TEARS,
&TORTURE

_ 33 Days in Kidnappers Den

Stephen Omeiza Ojapah

Author

Stephen Ojapah

Table of Contents

Dedication

To God Almighty who gave me a second chance in life and the opportunity to tell my story. To my late father whose sense of humour and love for reading has not departed from me; my mom who taught me the value of prayer. In a special way I dedicate this book to the good people of Gidan Mai Kambu, in the Catholic diocese of Katsina who gave me the opportunity to serve them. In a more special way, I dedicate this work to the Catholic Diocese of Sokoto.

Acknowledgements

This work has only been possible, thanks to the many people who have seen me develop in my public life. Sadly, this page will not be able to mention many of them, not because they did not contribute enough, but for want of space. Many people encouraged me to write about my experience. I started writing immediately after our release, but the trauma was too real for me to continue. I thank my bishop and mentor, Matthew Hassan Kukah, the priests and the religious of the Catholic Diocese of Sokoto for standing by us when we needed them most. My spiritual family is the Missionary Society of St Paul. I thank you all most warmly. My immediate family has been very instrumental in aiding my healing process.

My mother, Mrs. Maryamoh Ojapah, never stopped suggesting ways for me to improve, "Whatever good exercise you can engage in," she says, including prayer and writing.

My immediate brothers and sisters, Mary-Anne, Bibiana, Patrick and Boniface, have been wonderful in providing me with helpful information about what happened on the days we were with the kidnappers. All my cousins, to mention a few of them. Albert, Alphonsus, Fr Henry, Lawrence, Sr Jane Ojapah EHJ. Many I am not able to capture here; thank most sincerely. The fact that I've been able to write this far shows how far I've come. Father Cosmas Nwosu MSP has constantly reminded me to write about this experience, but I didn't stick to his advice to keep it short and brief.

When I got the recordings of the phone conversations between the bandits and the negotiator, I tried to translate some from the Hausa language to English. But I realised that it would take a lot more effort, so it was Ummie Hassan, (one of the victims of the incident) who, helped me. Although it was a very traumatic conversation, she managed to overcome the pain of reviewing the conversations about her 33 days in captivity. . In trying to contextualize this work, I wanted to obtain data on the killings between Boko Haram and banditry since the creation of Boko Haram, and I contacted Beacon Security and Intelligence (BSI) and Chasuth Intelligence (Chasuth). BSI generously granted me access to their data, but I had already received a response from Chasuth Intelligence—my sincere thanks to BSI. As a result, the data analysed here is exclusively that of Chasuth Intelligence. I would like to thank Tolu Ola-David for helping me understand the data and carry out the analysis professionally. When I finished this work, I sent it to my American mother, Mrs Tina Dirksen, for review. Her criticism and insights have made this a great piece of academic and pastoral literature.

Frs Evaristus Abu and Justin Dyikuk have been invaluable in providing me with their insights and comments. I am also grateful to Sr Esther Esawe - EHJ, Sr Cecilia Maundu - Focolarina, and Sr Jovita Ochi - SCS for their deep insights and reviews. I thank Sr. Susan Didam SSL and Mrs Charity Obetta for their valuable corrections. When Sr Nancy Gregory OP proof read the work, she added some dynamics I had not noticed. I'd like to thank Sr. Nancy for going through the work. I sincerely thank Father Oliver Okpara, Ummie Hassan and Hassan Fareed Hassan for giving me the energy to pull through when I needed it most in life—those horrible days of trekking with guns. God put you in my path to make this kidnapping less painful.

Lastly my appreciation also goes to Fr Moses Amune, MSP, and Mr Peter Maundu. To Fr Amune, thank you sincerely for helping me settle into the UK Mission so quickly. Your brotherly care is second to none. You never stopped enquiring about the work's progress and gave me space to work when needed. You are truly a brother and a friend. To Mr Peter Maundu, from the EU Business School in Geneva: THANK YOU. I wish I could say it louder in Swahili: Asante sana. You gave a brilliant look to my poor work. I am deeply grateful to you.

Preface

One of my greatest dreams in life was to write a book one day. But I had a big problem with the subject. I thought that I would have enough to write about after ten years working in the Diocese of Sokoto and having helped resolve numerous crises and conflicts between Muslims and Christians. At best, I thought I would write about the experiences of others, as I did in my Sunday Reflections on the Daily Trust News Papers. It is with sadness and joy that I am writing my first book about my personal life experience in the Diocese of Sokoto, which ended with a story of abduction. That story changed me forever; it completely redefined me because I now see life differently. Certain passages of Scripture seem more alive to me than before, in many ways, because of that experience.

It was difficult for me to start writing about this experience because every letter and every piece of writing caused me a lot of pain at first. I tried not to write about this experience because it reminded me of the darkest days of my human existence. After months of silence, I suddenly realized that one of the best ways to heal internally was to communicate this experience through writing. When I wrote about this experience, I saw myself walking along the bush path, in the dungeons, in the rain and the scorpion stings, not as a kidnapped victim again, but as a victor.

My whole life in the Diocese of Sokoto has been, in my opinion, very productive. I look back with great pride and a sense of fulfilment. I feel that I have not wasted my time working with the poor villagers of Gidan Mai Kambu. I am proud and happy to have had the time to work with Bishop Kukah and all the wonderful experiences communicated in the book were possible because of the support I received working with him. . He was a father and mentor par excellence. This book is a journey about Nigeria, but especially to the north of the country. For all other readers, (non-Nigerians), this is an opportunity to broaden their knowledge of a people far from their own country or continent, perhaps they or members of their family might one day live in Nigeria.

Foreword

Arrest, detention, threats, intimidation, torture, imprisonment and so on are often the strategies that dictators use to bring those opposed to them into line. Usually, when countries are under a dictatorship, military or civilian, these are the strategies they use to cow citizens or to command obedience. The stories of many nations are full of these phases of the lives of many citizens.

When detainees, or prisoners are released the world always awaits their stories, but of course, this all depends on the stature of the person in question. It also depends on the circumstances in which these people find themselves. Often, the state engages in psychological torture by denying you access to loved ones, denying you reading materials, access to print or electronic media. Denial of access to writing materials is often at the top of the list of violations. Naturally, the tyrant would never give you a chance to tell your story.

When Ngugi Wa Thiongo the famous writer was detained in the late 70s, he later published an account of his experience titled, Detained: A Writer's Prison Diary, in 1981. After the Rev. Martin Luther King Jr. was freed from detention after one week in Birmingham, USA, he published his searing book titled, A Letter from a Birmingham Jail, in 1963. He, like Ngugi had relied on toilet paper to write his letter. In his own case, he had used long hand to write the letter. When he came out of detention by the military regime, Wole Soyinka published his memoirs titled, The Man Died: Prison Notes of Wole Soyinka, in 1972. Nelson Mandela's Long Walk to Freedom gave a great account of his time in Robben Island and so on.

The book in your hands however is not exactly the same. Fr. Stephen Ojapah was not captured by the agents of the Nigerian State. He was not captured because of an offence he created. On the contrary, had it been left to his parishioners, the great work he was doing for them would have required that he be rewarded in another way as a sign of their love and appreciation. Rather, Fr. Ojapah, like thousands of his fellow countrymen and women, fell victim to a dysfunctional state which had been literally overrun by hordes of criminals and bandits running riot across the country. He and others like him are victims of a country that is unable to protect its citizens, security agencies that have, in some instances constitute a tag team with the bandits and kidnappers. No one knows if this story will ever be told.

The book in your hands tells a very sad story of how horrible things can and do happen to good people. Fr. Ojapah and his colleague, Fr. Oliver Okpara were serving in the Parish of Gidan Maikambu in the Kafur Local Government of Katsina state. They had and still enjoyed their services to their parishioners when their peace was suddenly invaded and their harmony sadly brought to an end. Together with two siblings, Ummie and Hassan who had come on a visit, they were violently taken away that night.

The book in your hands tells the story as best as they can try to recollect. Unlike the enemies of State that I have referred to above, they were abducted by people who did not know them and had perhaps nothing personal beyond their evil quest for money at all cost. The book already tells you the account of their experiences in the hands of these beasts, in human flesh. But as you will see, they were nowhere near any writing material. Under such a hostile environment and torture, you lose a sense of time. Indeed, they deserve our commendation that they survived to tell their story. Theirs is a story of faith and the courage of the human spirit. We the readers owe them a debt of gratitude and we thank Fr. Ojapah in particular for putting these thoughts down.

God's ways are truly not our ways (Is. 55: 8). Putting these stories behind, their lives have taken perhaps more fulfilling ways. While Fr. Ojapah has ended up doing pastoral work in the United Kingdom, Ummie and her brother are now studying in the Godfrey Okoye University in Enugu, thanks to a scholarship by the University. Fr. Oliver is back and doing pastoral work while waiting to go for a pilgrimage sometime in the near future, thanks to Aid to Church in Need.

Whatever God allows to happen has a purpose. We thank God that they have added their sufferings to the Cross that we pray will provide Nigeria's Redemption. Fr. Alphonsus Bello Yashim who was kidnapped was not lucky, neither did Michael Nnadi. They have joined the pantheon of the Martyrs of Nigeria. We believe that Nigeria's redemption is nearer than we can appreciate.

Most Rev. Matthew Hassan Kukah

Bishop, Diocese of Sokoto

Introduction

You owe the world a story at the end of every important mission. So said Bishop Kukah at the media launch of his latest book, Witness to Reconciliation. The book recounts his reconciliation experience between the Ogoni people and the Shell Oil Company in Rivers State under the presidency of Chief Olusegun Obasanjo. Having worked for ten years as a priest in some of the most challenging terrain in Nigeria, it is only reasonable that I should write about my unique experience. It is a source of research and inspiration for future generations.

My humble beginnings in the book attempt to illustrate the average life of a Nigerian child and family, the hardships many families face, and the fact that I did not escape as a child. Difficult as they maybe, these difficulties do not prevent children from reaching the pinnacle of their dreams, wherever they may be. The first part also divides Nigeria into two categories: the haves and the have-nots. These two categories of people coexist in most cases. While one flies away for the simplest reasons, the other passes through the worst potholes on the country roads. Why do some people live in darkness without electricity while others have access to numerous alternative energy sources?

This book recounts my humble beginnings in Gidan Mai Kambu, engaging the Muslim and Christian communities in many projects, including boreholes, the peaceful resolution of the problem of captive girls and boys and extremist clerics, among others. This experience will teach the reader more about the paradox that has befallen Nigeria—poor governance and the many layers that have contributed to this scourge. Fifteen years of data provided by Chasuth Intelligent Limited are analysed using graphs to show the progression of the deteriorating situation. This puts my abduction situation into context. I am just one of the few that have come out with their stories. There are legions of us, each with a unique and painful story of tears and torture.

The shortest chapter in the book; is chapter six, it is a significant event in the body of the entire story; and I decided to make it brief because of the significance of this short conversation. It was a text that foreshadowed my abduction and death. Maybe if I had run away, I wouldn't have been kidnapped. Maybe if the police had been more active, they would have traced the owner of the number. A lot of maybes. In all, I'm trying to explain how 'cheap' life has become in Nigeria and many other parts of the world.

That text message prepared me for the worst when it happened. I was ready to pay a high price because I had been informed. So, they arrived, and we embarked on a perilous journey to nowhere for two days. We went through some difficult times and places, but thank God it's all history now.

Four of us were involved in this ordeal: Fr Oliver Okpara, Ummie Hassan; Hassan Farid Hassan and myself. The Hassan's family from Sokoto are long-time family friends of mine. We all went for a funeral in the southern part of Nigeria. On our way back, there was the sad incidence of the stoning to death of Deborah Samuel in Sokoto, and for some days, Sokoto State was boiling as a result of the religious tension and violence. The Hassans all stayed back in our parish waiting for the situation to be calm, when things got better, their mother left to Sokoto, and Ummie and Hassan where to follow soon. A day after their mother left for Sokoto the next day the terrorists struck.

The Readers will see what daily life is like with the kidnappers. The telephone conversation that got us out was frightening and traumatic. I would never have believed that anyone could survive such a situation. Amid all these terrible situations, providence turned this tragedy into something good for Fr Oliver's father and my elder sister. Among the many things life has taught me is the virtue of patience in dealing with kidnappers. You will never remain the same after experiencing the horrors of a handful of people among the hundreds of thousands who suffer torture and tears every day in many parts of the world, particularly in Nigeria.

Chapter One

Humble Beginning

Epic things start with small steps. Pay respect to your beginnings. And if you're just starting out, know that it's just okay to be sucky. To be small. To be messy and chaotic. Just make sure to never ever stop dreaming

Vishen Lakhiani

"Wake up, my wife is delivered of a male child." those were my father's words to neighbours the night he went to the hospital and discovered his wife had given birth to a male child. I'm the fifth born but the first male child in my family. In Nigeria, male children are seen as a sure sign of stability in a woman's marriage. In some Nigerian cultures, a woman is not considered to have given birth to a child if all her children are female. I suppose my father was locked up in that world at the time. Needless to say, there was a lot of joy in the family. I wasn't there to explain that part, but my mother told me it was a celebration, and I believe her.

I was born in Yola, in the State of Adamawa, in northern Nigeria. I had a happy childhood with loving parents until my parents got divorced in 1990, and we sadly had to stay with our mom alone without dad. An experience that no child should go through in life. My mother then became the 'iron' lady of the house. She brought us up according to the strictest rules of prayer, study and work. Growing up with my mother was the most 'difficult' part of my life, but looking back, all I can say is thank you, Mum, for everything you've been to us. During my childhood, like many children in Nigeria, I sold things to earn money to support the family. I used to assist my mom in selling wrappers. I also trekked 30 miles to school every day. My mother made sure we excelled by providing everything she could to support us as a family.

A Typical Nigerian Family

Nigeria is a very multi-ethnic and multi-religious country. With 371 ethnic groups, over 500 languages and English as the official language, a typical Nigerian family varies according to social class, ethnic group and religion. But I will provide some basic groupings that should fairly explain the dynamics of so many Nigerian families. In my view, Nigeria can be divided into two broad categories: the haves and the have-nots. Nigeria is a country of over 200 million people. In its November 2022 report, the National Bureau of Statistics (NBS) states that 133 million Nigerians live in multidimensional poverty. This represents 63.4% of the population. Less than 40% of the country's wealth is controlled by the haves. Despite this, Nigeria is considered the happiest country in Africa (World Happiness Report 2024).

Nigeria's haves are essentially the sons and daughters of politicians, a few very lucky business tycoons, many retired senior civil servants, and many big entrepreneurs who have established their businesses in violence-free areas. These Nigerian families are Christian or Muslim and belong to any tribe or language. They have access to everything in life. Alternative energy sources, such as generators and solar power, are available because not all the country has stable electricity. The *haves*, can attend the choicest schools in Nigeria and worldwide. Some of them have small families of 5 or 4 children, while others have up to twenty-seven (27) children, and others forty (40) children with numerous wives. This number of children is a source of pride for these wealthy Nigerians.

I will focus mainly on the *have-nots* because they represent the majority of Nigerians. It's from them that the insurgents are recruited. According to a UNICEF report: over 10.5 million children are out of school in Nigeria. These numbers belong to the children of the '*Have Not's'*. The 'Yahoo' boys (A group of young desperate boys specialized in Internet fraud) equally come from this grouping. The number of out-of-school children is higher than many European countries and certain glacial regions. For example, it is higher than the population of Switzerland, Finland and Norway. Yet these *'Have Nots'* lead stable lives, with the father supporting the family and the mothers helping out as best as they can.

Farming remains the main form of employment for the *'Have Nots,'* but very few of them take up mechanised and commercial farming. Those who do engage in commercial or mechanised farming are well-to-do or wealthy people. There are also many other small businesses, such as construction, manufacturing local products, selling local products, teaching, medical activities (nurses, pharmacies, doctors, lawyers, Sharia courts, etc.), and so on. In some northern states such as Sokoto, Kano, Zamfara, Katsina and Jigawa, which are very Islamic, polygamy is widespread, as are large families. A poor man who can't afford to feed himself properly will have four wives and up to 25 children. Don't ask me how they feed themselves; your opinion is as good as mine. In the northern states, some women are not allowed to work in accordance with Islamic teaching. You don't particularly see the wives of the rich adopting this lifestyle.

The average Nigerian family does not know what it means to live on one hour of electricity a day. Many communities have never seen an electricity pole in their lives. Most average families don't know what it means to eat three times a day. The ideal is a full meal. The cost of food rose by 2000% between May 2023 and July 2024, making ordinary families poorer and unable to buy food from the market; the price of fuel has risen astronomically since the start of President Bola Tinubu's administration.

Marriage and family are treasures in Nigeria. Family values are held in high esteem. Above all, religion is very well celebrated in Nigeria. Christians and Muslims take their faith very seriously. I come from a mixed family; my mother was a Muslim before she married my father, and my cousins are all children of her Muslim sisters and brothers. My maternal grandmother died a proud Muslim, but she always called me to say those prayers that I used to say while wearing those glorious vestments (chasubles for Holy Mass, in this case). Thus, many Nigerian Christians and Muslims share a common family. Some parts of the country are more tolerant of a mixed family with religious differences. The south-west, for example, is very tolerant of religious differences, while the northwest is less so.

Education and out-of-school children

Education is a major asset in Nigeria. Although the country has more than ten million out-of-school children, there are millions of highly educated Nigerians in rich and poor communities alike. After the civil war 1970, the Nigerian government closed down faith-based schools and hospitals and 'nationalised' them to the detriment of their quality. The government took over the schools and mismanaged them. This mismanagement stems from the teaching conditions, the lack of motivated teachers and the absence of supervision. After the moratorium on private and Catholic schools was lifted, the Church returned with the highest academic excellence. Across the country. In the north of the country. Catholic schools remained the best, topping the table every year in the national exams. Holy Family School, Sokoto, Dominican College, Gusau, St Vincent Ferrer Malumfashi, St Peter's Minor Seminary, Yola (my alma mater) and Loyola Jesuit College, Abuja have topped the lists of the best schools in Nigeria for the past ten years. None of these schools receive any financial support from the government. Anambra State is an exception to the rule: Peter Obi's government returned all schools to the Church and passed a law to support all faith-based schools.

The north of the country uses the Almajiri education system. This is a Koranic school designed to teach young boys about Islam and the Koran. Over time, this system has been abused and mismanaged, resulting in millions of children roaming the streets of Nigeria. These kids, who number in the hundreds of thousands, primarily live in the country's north are constantly seen on the streets begging for food.

Chapter Two

A Priest till The End

"John Paul II was a priest till the end."
Joseph Cardinal Ratzinger 2005

I was ordained in June 2013. Since ordination, I worked in Gidan Mai Kambu, a small farming community in Katsina State, between December 2013 and May 2023. The community is located in the Kafur Local Government Area of Katsina State, in northwest Nigeria. My pastoral ministry occurred during the presidency of two important presidents in the history of Nigeria, Goodluck Ebele Jonathan and Muhammadu Buhari. These two presidents have played an important role in shaping my pastoral ministry in northern Nigeria. In the course of my work, my readers will learn why and how these two presidents have influenced my pastoral ministry in northern Nigeria.

The parishioners of Gidan Mai Kambu are mainly peasants whose poverty prevents them from engaging in large-scale commercial farming. Many of them start begging for food as early as January each year, during a farming season that begins in June and ends in October. The first few years of my priesthood were very formative, as I had to relearn the basics of life and relationships. I had to remember my seminary formation to guide me in my ministry at Gidan Mai Kambu.

I began the first three months of my work with the late Fr. Stephen Achi, MSP. May God rest his soul. Those first three months of being his assistant taught me a lot of patience and humility. I learnt to follow my leader, even if I feel I'm better. In the future I will find the time to say a few words about that great priest, who taught me a lot in life despite my short stay with him. After his departure from Gidan Mai Kambu in April 2014, I became the pastor of that community until my unfortunate incidence of the kidnapping in May of 2022.

This work is an attempt to examine the gentle power of the priest in the community of Muslims and Christians, living in the 21st Century. It is also an attempt to ex-ray the multi-layered intrigues that have brought Nigeria to its knees: these intrigues include: Religious intolerance, unemployment, tribalism, ISIS-backed insurgency, injustice, and the names behind the numbers I will provide in subsequent chapters. The last ten years of my life in Gidan Mai Kambu were marked by enough moments of drama and interesting phenomena, all of which I am eternally grateful to God.

Pastoral Life

When we first arrived in Malumfashi with Fr. Stephen Achi, some pastoral council members were asked to come and welcome us at Malumfashi. When I went out to receive them, I was surprised to see how many people had come to welcome us. There were fifteen of them. We greeted each other, and then I took them into the parlour, where we exchanged pleasantries for some time and wished each other well. After about thirty minutes of warm greetings and introductions, Father Achi, the parish priest, wished them well in our newly found relationship in working together. When I accompanied them to the car for their departure, I was amazed to see the 15 people neatly packed into a starlet vehicle. Ordinarily, the seating capacity of such a car is four, and five is actually considered to be overload. And yet here they are, crammed into a four-person vehicle. When I started working at Gidan Mai Kambu, I realised he was the only person in the village who owned a car.

Mai Kambu is a poor and humble community. My daily routine ranged from morning Mass to farm visits and home visits. These visits kept me very busy from morning to night. During my stay, I discovered that water was a devastating human need, with many parishioners travelling tens of kilometres to fetch water. A community like Gidan Musa depends on a seasonal river for its annual water supply. Once the river dries up, there is no water available in the community until the next rainy season. I spent most of my time getting support from friends and missions to build wells in many Muslim and Christian communities.

Relationship with the Bishop, Priests and Religious

Every establishment is built around the personality of a leader. The great men who have built companies that have lasted for centuries must be part of our daily studies, for they have much to teach us. I am sure many people will try to give varied accounts of their experience working with Nigeria's most iconic religious cleric over the past 50 years. Bishop Matthew Hassan Kukah is a phenomenon that needs to be extensively researched by social scientists.

My relationship with him went beyond the formal relationship between a bishop and a priest, but certainly that of a father and a son. To me, he was a father with whom I was proud to disagree, without fear of being punished or judged by him. I personally challenged his decisions on several issues, and the understanding father that he is, he never took these challenges as personal attacks. He created an atmosphere of solidarity among colleagues in the diocese. He is a man of many stories, deep insights and extraordinary surprises. It's sometimes difficult to know exactly what makes him happy. But there's one thing that I've realised doesn't surprise him: hard work, and someone with good concentration in his or her work. He goes out of his way to support a priest or a sister; who commits himself/herself to his/her work.

And what is more surprising is that he will go out of his way, again and again, to support a priest who is not measuring up to the job. For me, Bishop Kukah is an extravagant father who celebrates the return of his prodigal sons and daughters. All of us priests in Sokoto have experienced this part of him, much to our surprise.

The priests and religious of Sokoto were my immediate colleagues. The last ten years of work in the diocese would not have been worthwhile without their friendship. We had real moments of laughter and shared sorrows. We stood by each other, especially when insecurity increased. The deaths of our seminarian Michael Nnadi and Father Alphonsus Bello Yashim at the hands of bandits brought out the best in our collaboration. Overall, life was easier and happier because priests and religious created a support network for each other.

Mai Kambu Sustainable Socioeconomic Development Initiative

The Maikambu initiative started operating in Gidan Mai Kambu on 16 December 2016, with financial support from Dr (Mrs) Charity Obetta and technical support from Fr Patrick Etuk MSP. As parish priest of Gidan Mai Kambu, I coordinated the initiative from 2016 to 2023.

Mai Kambu is a small village located in Kafur Local Government Area of Katsina State in Nigeria, with a population of over two thousand people. The people of Mai Kambu and the surrounding villages are primarily farmers. Their main crops are rice, beans, maize, sorghum, onions, tomatoes, pepper and okra. There are a few small traders and skilled handiwork workers.

Vocational training is not fashionable, and farming is still based mainly on non-mechanical approaches. For full-time farmers, the cultivation method is certainly not good enough to guarantee a profitable harvest, as many practice subsistence farming just to live for the next day and not enough to save for a rainy day. It's almost expected that in August, almost everywhere, food becomes very scarce. Certainly, the method and scale of farming cannot guarantee food all year round.

The average farmer lives on less than a dollar a day and, in many places, on less than two dollars a week. It is this difficult situation that has led the community of Gidan Mai Kambu and some neighbouring communities who have identified similar or worse situations to come together and see how an organised group or cooperative can reduce poverty in their area and create opportunities for themselves and access government or international funds to reduce poverty and improve living standards.

Development activities and projects are still considered to be the responsibility of the government. In some cases, people at the grassroots level are often excluded from the equation, even regarding issues that affect their development. Where such programmes exist, they are generally not implemented or are poorly implemented. The programme sought to be all-inclusive, covering everything from members training to utilizing professionals and experts in various fields of study, including business, contemporary farming practices, and skill development.

The living conditions and lives of the people in these communities revolve around their farms and families and can be described using the following three cycles.

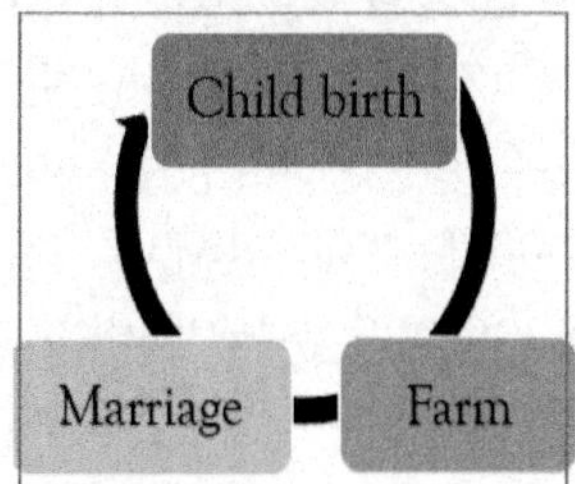
Child birth
Marriage
Farm

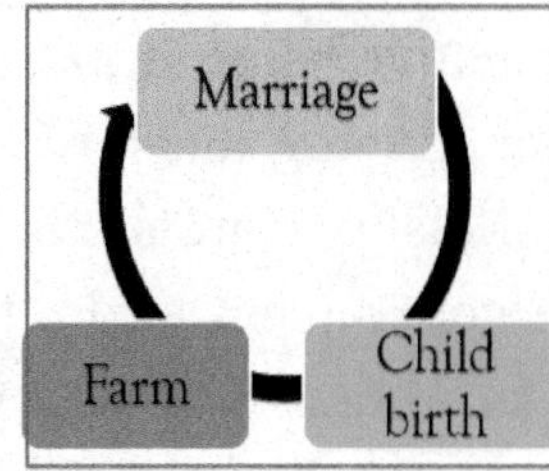
Marriage
Farm
Child birth

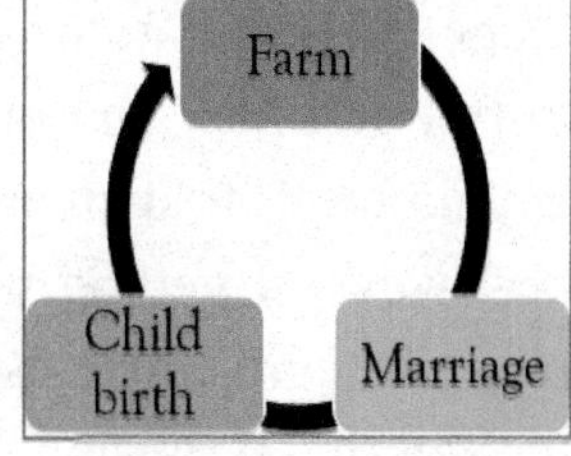
Farm
Child birth
Marriage

This is certainly not the sign of a community ripe for liberation. Education is present, but on a minimal scale and with little importance, and when it is present, the quality is appalling. To help these communities, we needed to start where they can better understand and appreciate the efforts of governments, donor agencies or NGOs. With greater financial viability and a better life around them, the need for access to good education will increase. The communities concerned are socially deprived of infrastructure such as schools, hospitals, lighting, drinking water, and good roads in these areas will be a luxury. Villagers like those in Gidan Garba Da dai spend almost 50% of their resources getting their agricultural produce to the tarmac roads that will take them to market. With better roads, they will not spend even 2% of what they currently spend on transport alone. Every year, the initiative helps farmers who have little money to buy fertiliser and other farming tools. My last ten years working among the Christian and Muslim communities have been finding the best ways of getting the government to do its job and getting other organisations to invest in Gidan Mai Kambu to make life better through the provision of good schools, potable water, electricity and many other creative things.

Working in Northern Nigeria

In 2021, I participated in a media campaign called 'Appeal to Bandits.' It was a six-month programme on Radio Nigeria, mainly in Hausa. Hausa and Fulani are the two languages used by the bandits to communicate. Any news broadcast in these two languages reaches them. Shiekh Maraya and I were the main presenters of this programme. We spoke directly to the bandits via the radio and asked them to bring peace to the country. Obviously, the message got through. They told me the news. They asked me if I was the one talking to them in the media. I said yes.

Insecurity has simply become the latest of the countless challenges facing northern Nigeria. The whole country has different problems.

But my immediate context is the north of the country. That's where I served for ten years. In general, the northwest of the country is predominantly Muslim. The southeast of the country is predominantly Christian. The Christian minority in the north faces structural and physical violence, both covert and overt. This violence can take the form of denial of land for church building, admission to higher institutions, employment opportunities, etc. Interestingly, the things that Christians complain about are also the things that Muslims in the Southeast complain about (Golden Rule: Igbo Muslims and Hausa Christian, Stephen Ojapah 2021).

But the greatest challenges have been faced by minorities in the north, who have had to deal with constant attacks by bandits or Boko Haram. Bandits in Nigeria, Kebbi, Zamfara, Sokoto, Katsina, Kaduna and Plateau have destroyed hundreds of villages. (Kukah Centre: NADP Reports, 2022). These security problems have been part of our daily lives in the North since 2010 when Boko Haram began its attacks. It is in this context of coercion, fear and the threat of death and destruction that I ministered in the Catholic Diocese of Sokoto.

Chapter Three

Nigeria - A Traumatised Nation

The World Interfaith Harmony Week aligns with KAICIID's Vision of building a world filled with respect, understanding, cooperation, justice, peace, and reconciliation; we strive to put an end to the exploitation of religion to condone oppression, violence and conflict."

Zuhair Al-Harthi, Secretary General KAICIID

Interfaith dialogue

The Diocese of Sokoto is in the middle of four Muslim-dominated states: Sokoto, Zamfara, Kebbi and Katsina. Today, Katsina no longer exists, leaving Kebbi, Sokoto and Zamfara. Naturally, I lived among a large majority of Muslims. Christians don't have many opportunities and are significantly disadvantaged, so I saw the need to engage the Muslim community in the process of friendship and support. My love for dialogue led the bishop to officially appoint me a priest in charge of inter-religious dialogue and ecumenism for the diocese of Sokoto. I held this post from 2016 to 2023 when I finally left the diocese. This work took me to the four corners of the world and every region of Nigeria. I met all the main emirs and religious leaders in the north and the country. I was particularly close to Alhaji Abdullahi Rabbe Hakimin Kafur, the traditional leader of the Local Government, who died at 96. He treated me as an equal but also as a grandson. As an equal because, he knew I was the spiritual leader of a large Christian community. But also like a grandson because I could only be close to his grandchildren.

I developed a serious friendship with Alhaji Rabbe, which paid off in many ways. I visited his palace several times, and he also visited me several times, including at church. His most notable visit was when he came to church to join our parishioners in celebrating the feast of St Patrick, the patron saint of the parish. Alhaji Rabbe, a devout Muslim, remained in the church from start to finish, a remarkable gesture of deep friendship and acceptance on his part.

I also belong to some of the most formidable interfaith groups, both inside and outside the country. I am a member of the Interfaith Dialogue Forum for Peace (IDFP) and a member of the King Abdulla bin Abdul Aziz Centre for Intercultural and Interfaith Dialogue (KAICIID). (KAICIID). I have been a facilitator for the Tony Blair Foundation for Global Change, a member of the North West Forum of the Institute for Peace and Conflict Resolution (IPCR) and a consultant for the Kukah Centre on several projects. These groups and organisations have enhanced my skills in working with the Muslim community in northern Nigeria, as I have dealt with many issues of conflict between Christians and Muslims that could have escalated into violence if not properly managed.

Cases of conversions that generated tensions and challenges

Working in this type of environment presented many challenges, the most important being the cases of forced conversion of Christian girls and minors that I had to deal with directly. During my ten years of experience in Sokoto, Zamfara, Kebbi and Katsina States, there were hundreds of cases of forced conversion of girls and boys. Many of these cases have caused an outcry and attracted the international community's attention. But the vast majority of these cases have gone unreported. I want to highlight three cases that never entered the public domain and never would have. The real names have been changed to preserve their privacy.

Rukayya

I had only been in the parish for three months when the parents of Rukkaya, a 17-year-old girl, came to beg me to accompany them to the Hakimis' palace to get their daughter back, who they said had been missing for a week. Credible information showed them that Rukkaya was at the Hakimis' (traditional chiefs') palace. It was the first time I had witnessed what I had heard about in the media. I put on my clerical dress and accompanied the parents to the palace. When we arrived at the palace, the Hakimi (traditional chief) greeted us and asked us why we were there. The father stood up and said that his daughter, like many others, was in his house and had converted to Islam. Without discussion, the Hakimi demanded that the girl be brought out. I was shocked when he confirmed that Rukkaya was indeed in his custody.

A few minutes later, Rukkaya came out and sat beside us. Her father was a catechist in one of the churches in the Diocese of Sokoto, and I was her parish priest. The Hakimi questioned Rukkaya in front of us all, and asked her if she knows us? By then, the poor girl's name had already been changed to Maryam: 'Maryam or Rukkaya raised her head and looked at me, her father and the few elders who were with her and said NO. She doesn't know us. Rukkaya's father was furious, angry and ready to blow the roof of the palace, but we managed to calm him down. It was a lesson in humility. I was shocked beyond words, wondering what they could have done to Rukkaya to make her disown us all. Rukkaya sits at the front roll of the church every Sunday, so I see her at Mass every Sunday. I've come to realise that this is a normal pattern in 99% of the cases of forced conversion of young Christian girls that I've dealt with. They are led to deny their family members and friends. I have been following this case in Katsina State and have made no progress. Rukkaya is in her eleventh year of 'marriage' to the man she was made to marry, and she has three children.

Jamima

I was on holiday at Christmas 2016 when the catechist of one of the outstation churches called to tell me that his member had gone for a home visit at Christmas and still hadn't returned, and hadn't for a fortnight and that the whole community had gone back to look for Jamima. I was on holidays and couldn't follow the case. I asked a visiting priest in the church to help me follow the case. The visiting priest rolled up his sleeves and started to do the right thing. He gathered the local chiefs and relatives and went straight to the Hakimi palace. Unfortunately, Jamima was discovered there, and the same procedures were followed as in the case of Rukkaya, where the girl was brought in and asked if she knew the people looking for her. Predictably, the girl said NO, and once she denies knowing her parents in this way, that's usually the end of the story. We've seen it happen time and time again. Jamima's case had a happy ending, because six months after her disappearance, she surprisingly returned home. The hypnosis ended quickly in her case. When she returned, I contacted her and asked her to tell me what had happened. This is what she told me.

"I was on my way to my aunt's house after Christmas mass. The bike that took me said he had no change to give me when I gave him N500, so he collected the money to give me N400, and that's all I remember, Father. The next thing I remember was I was on a man's bed in a house I couldn't recognise. When I saw myself on his bed, I quickly realised two things: 1. That I wasn't dead and 2. That I was in trouble. From then on, I started following the instructions as usual so he wouldn't realise I'd come to my senses. At night, I told him I was going to fetch water from the streams, and when I went out, I followed a bush track and found myself in a place where I could ask for help.

Jamima's case is quite good because it ended quickly and without drama.

Jamilu

This is the story of a 14-year-old boy who went to school and never came back. His parents came to see me and asked me to intervene, thinking I knew where their son was. I joined them in making a statement to the police and local authorities. Later that day, the parents told me their son was staying with a local Islamic teacher. The teacher said that Jamilu had converted to Islam. This time, I drew on the friendship I already had with Alhaji Rabbe, the late Hakimi of the region, and wrote him a letter asking that the boy be returned to his parents, as he had not reached the constitutional age to make a decision on his own. Surprisingly enough, Alhaji Rabbe ordered the Islamic teacher to return the boy to his parents. Again, this was fairly easy and rare, as most cases of this kind never end well.

Magaji Mato and Alhaji Negebu

Father Stephen: Hello, Sir. My name is Father Stephen, and this is part of an in-depth interview and research for the book I've written on the challenges facing minorities in Nigeria, particularly in the north of the country. Can we find out more about you?

Barr. Magaji: My name is Magaji Mato Ibrahim, SAN. I come from the Catholic Diocese of Kano.

Father Stephen: Wonderful; I'm delighted to meet you, Mr. SAN. How long have you been the Senior Advocate of Nigeria?

Barr: I've been practising for 17 years.

Father. Stephen: That's impressive! And your entire legal career has been spent in the metropolis of Kano? Or have you worked outside Kano?

Barr: My work has taken me to several states. I worked at Kwara State, in Ilorin. I was initially posted to the Police Headquarters as a legal officer. Then, I found myself working in a chamber to keep abreast of the practice of law, but I asked, for personal reasons, to be allowed to participate in the practices of that office. The senior partner allowed me to, and I worked with him for a few months when another office asked me to join because of the two relationships the two chambers shared.

While I was there, I had a lot of opportunities. The office was busy with election petitions, and I travelled from state to state, where we dealt with election issues. I was also involved in the election cases involving Adams Oshiomhole and Professor Osahime at the time in Edo State. I was also involved in the legal battle of the Ekiti State case involving Mr. Oni and Fayemi, the current governor, but at that time, he was a member of the Action Party while Mr. Oni was a member of the PDP. Fortunately, I was involved in all these electoral affairs in Lagos, Illorin and Kano. After my service, my senior partner, who was also SAN then, asked me to stay, but I politely declined. Perhaps fate was pushing me to return to Kano, and against his wishes, I had to move to Kano after my compulsory one-year service. Reluctantly, I didn't want to join him, but after a while, I agreed, and here's what happened.

I practised with him for two years, during which time I got married in 2008. In 2009, I had to submit my letter of resignation because I was asked to work with the former Attorney General of the Federation, Professor Ignatius Ayua SAN, who hails from Benue State. When I arrived in Abuja, I didn't like the nature of my work: I was passionate about practice, but he was essentially advisory. I returned to Kano and opened my own practice in 2009; even though I had already registered my office in 2008, the practice started in 2009. That's how I started, and I've continued to grow until today.

Fr. Stephen: I'd like to congratulate you once again on your appointment as SAN, but I'm curious to know how you feel about it. How do you feel about it?

Barr: It's a great achievement. For me, it's the best thing that could happen to a practising solicitor because it's the pinnacle. At this stage, reaching this level at this age is a grace from God. Usually, people will tell you that you've worked hard, but God's grace also counts in hard work.

Throughout my years of practice, I have shown commitment and dedication. I didn't focus my practice on the purely commercial aspect, i.e., the monetary aspect, but I was passionate about finding solutions for my clients. When a client entrusted me with a case, I was always particularly motivated to see it through to the end; I always wanted to find solutions to my client's problems. So, most of the time, I found myself doing pro bono, i.e., dealing with cases without necessarily billing the client, because I thought my passion had taken me far. In most cases, my friends had to remind me that people who didn't have the same level of experience as I had also applied. So, I applied at the beginning of 2022, and it has been so good so far. I'm where I am.

To the glory of God, I feel happy and accomplished, but I also believe that this is only the beginning of the journey toward a bigger world.

Fr. Stephen: I think I should ask more questions about the pro bono activity, but I think that will come in the following questions. Again, congratulations to you and your family. I know that as a lawyer, there are cases that you call your most famous. Can you tell us about some of those cases that you are incredibly proud of as a lawyer and their importance to our national development?

Barr. Magaji: I have handled several cases. In fact, I tried to analyse the cases in my office and found that in the High Court alone, I prosecuted over 400 cases. In the Court of Appeal, I handled 80 cases; in the Supreme Court, I handled 20 cases, which is a big deal. There are also cases that deal with classic issues and have a historical context.

I can name a few. I dealt with a case, the first since I started working in my office, which concerned a man who had been kidnapped in Kano State, at Kwali market, to be precise. He was touring our area and talking to some lawyers, but I noticed that he looked even more desperate every time he came back, devastated and frustrated. I was worried and decided to ask my colleague what the problem was. He told me the whole story and the steps he had taken. I didn't agree with them. You can't go to the police officers to get your money back. Luckily for him, he was there when I was making my contributions, and he asked me to pursue the matter, which I did. I got a judgment at the High Court of Kano State on 30 June 2009, the same day my first child (Suleiman) was born. I felt it was a reward from God. The young man had no money, but I volunteered to help him. The case went to every court in Nigeria and even to the Supreme Court, where I won. But before the case reached the Supreme Court, we had to obtain the personal assets of the man involved and attach them to the case because the other party involved had died, but we were able to see the case through to the end.

Another significant encounter was the case I handled for my community. At the time, I was just a young child when a rich man from Kano State, in collaboration with a village chief, seized a piece of land belonging to my community and another belonging to my father; it was a substantial piece of land of over 250 hectares. At the time, we were ignorant and childish, but I remember perfectly what my fellow villagers went through: some were arrested, detained and tortured, while others lost their lives because of this land. We were all powerless, but there was an Irish priest at the time, the Reverend Father Micheal Waters. He was the parish priest of this village, and out of compassion and pity, he did everything he could to secure the services of a lawyer. This was in the 80s (1985 or 86). But I noticed something after I became a lawyer.

I asked for this file and went to see the lawyer who had already become a judge at the Federal High Court in Asaba. I got in touch with him and told him of my intentions. It took him some time to agree and allow me access to the file. I looked at the file in detail and felt that the case had not been handled properly or had been compromised, but when I saw that the case was 30 years old and time-barred (too long), I didn't have enough confidence in my ability to progress or complete the case. He had them arrested again as if his plan was to take back the whole community because it wasn't one of those they had confiscated at the time. I got a call from the village in 2014, and he told me the whole story. I rushed to the command post where my people were being held, which caused serious problems for them. Fortunately for me, I fought and defended the case all the way to the High Court, and, in the end, my men were found not guilty, and we were released and acquitted. After all that, he was disappointed, so he got his lawyer and brought a civil action against my people for that piece of land, claiming it belonged to him. I wasn't confident about taking him to court because so much time had passed. So, I took the opportunity to file a counterclaim, which meant that this small piece and the one that they had did not belong to them.

The High Court didn't like my claim. It insisted that the land belonged to them. I appealed and had no difficulty in quashing the High Court documents. All the lands were returned to the people.

I was a child in my community when this conflict broke out, but there was nothing I could do then. God had the patience to raise me to a level where I can now be useful to my people. It was a great experience, and there's nothing better than that. Some of my fellow citizens told me that they had added another name to mine, that of Musa (Moses), who led the people of Israel out of Egypt, and I did the same for them. It was a party without limits. Even though the case is still pending before the Supreme Court, he has always complained, but I know that by the grace of God, we will win.

Fr. Stephen: So, you're saying that Nabegu is appropriating land not only from your community but also from others?

Barr: No, I can't say because I don't know if it's the same person taking land in other communities, but I do know that in my community, he has taken land not only from us but also from other families.

Fr. Stephen: Generally speaking, you kept mentioning that the police were used to harass people. Was it because the police weren't objective or interested in the truth? And again, was it only the Kano police or the general police of the federation that was compromised in this case?

Barr.: With all due respect to the Nigerian police, we all know that sometimes, when we talk about them, we don't hit the nail on the head. Most Nigerian police officers, though not all, tend to overlook objectivity in cases involving money when the individual has the means to pay.

Imagine, for example, that the Nigerian police arrest a culprit and detain him because of a dispute over the ownership of a piece of land. If you look at the situation from a legal point of view, you'll see that they don't even have the power to do that because the man kept saying that the land belonged to him and that my people were against it, so it's up to the court to decide, not the police.

At the time, in Kano, I didn't know exactly where he had found them because I was very young, but he used them to harass and intimidate my people, who stood their ground and said that no one could take their property away from them. I don't know the nature of the petition he filed against my people that made the police think they had the right to come. Maybe he lied to them and said the land belonged to him, and the others were trespassers. He probably portrayed the situation in such a way as to make it look criminal, but if there had been a proper investigation, they should have realised there was nothing criminal about it; it was just a dispute. Some were arrested at the market, while others were working on the farm, and so on. You must realise that the 'locals' shudder when they hear the word 'police.' When they arrested them, they detained and tortured them. Other people who saw this said that even if it were the last thing they had, they would not let go of the land. And many of my people died in the struggle of defending their land.

Fr. Stephen: Let me go back to the previous case you said you dealt with when you said you had gone back to check the file and realised it had been compromised. I don't think the Nabegu you mentioned is the one who confiscated the land, or is he the same person?

Barr.: No, Nabegu is a family name. I remember that his father was still very much alive at the time. Aminu Nabegu is Nagebu's first son. According to the information I have gathered, it was the real Nabegu who did it. He lied to them, telling them that the government wanted the land; they wanted to build businesses and employ their children there. Still, they refused, saying that they couldn't hand over their land to the government because it was their only means of survival, so he did everything he could to suppress them. It was later, after the people had protested that he declared that the land should be given back to the people, but the village chief flatly refused to do so. After their deaths, Aminu Nabegu took over from his father, and even then, I think he knew about it because he was his father's eldest son.

Chapter Four

A Nation In Paradox

A recent leaflet dropped on Nagasaki contained a grim poem: "In April Nagasaki was all flowers. In August, it will all be flame showers."

Paul Glynn: A Song for Nagasaki

Nigeria, a nation blessed with abundant natural resources and a vibrant mosaic of cultures, faces a seemingly intractable paradox. Despite its immense wealth, the country faces a pervasive challenge: widespread insecurity. Kidnappings for ransom, violent attacks by extremist groups and inter-communal clashes have become a tragic reality for too many Nigerians. This chapter examines the complex socio-political landscape that has fuelled this situation to shed light on the root causes and evolving nature of insecurity in Nigeria between 2009 and 2024.

Discovering the facets of insecurity

Insecurity in Nigeria takes many forms. Boko Haram, a militant Islamist group, has been wreaking havoc in the north-east of the country for the past 15 years, carrying out bomb attacks, mass kidnappings and large-scale violence against civilians (Omenma, Onyishi and Okolie, 2020). Ethnic oil groups in the Niger Delta region, which has vast oil resources, have resorted to pipeline sabotage and attacks on oil installations to secure a fair share of the oil wealth. While acts of piracy and kidnappings of oil workers have declined considerably over the years, oil theft continues to increase, affecting the national economy, which is primarily based on oil exploration. In addition, the country is faced with an increasing number of kidnappings for ransom and acts of banditry, which are gradually destroying public security and the daily lives of ordinary Nigerians. Consequently, this continues to erode the confidence of the citizenry in the ability of the government to discharge its primary responsibility of providing for the security and welfare of the people (Section 14(2) (b) of the Constitution of the Federal Republic of Nigeria 1999).

The ramifications of insecurity on human life

The humanitarian price paid by the Nigerian people for the existence of insecurity in the country is enormous. Thousands of people have been killed in brawls, while many have been displaced from their homes and ancestral lands. The trauma, violent attacks, kidnappings and constant fear cast a long shadow over the country. Beyond the immediate human suffering, insecurity stifles economic development, discourages investment and impedes progress.

This chapter, therefore, aims to untangle the web of factors at the root of the country's security crisis. By examining socioeconomic disparities, political instability and the emergence of violent actors, I will highlight the increase in insecurity since 2009 and attempt to propose solutions as an essential step towards forging a more secure and peaceful future for Nigeria.

Socioeconomic factors: The clay of rising insecurity

Currently estimated at 200 million, Nigeria's population has outstripped economic development. The consequences of this are as multiple as they are complex, wreaking havoc on the country's national security. (Walker, Robert. 2016). Nigeria's population explosion, which should be a blessing in disguise, has created many problems that contribute significantly to the national security crisis.

Too many people chasing limited resources creates immense pressure on available resources. Basic necessities such as food, water and shelter are becoming increasingly scarce. Unemployment rates, particularly among young people, remain very high. According to a 2023 report by the National Bureau of Statistics, the combined unemployment rate and time-related underemployment as a share of the labour force (LU2) was 15.5% in the second quarter of 2023. (National Statistics Office, Nigerian Youth Unemployment Rate 2023). This lack of economic opportunity breeds frustration and despair, creating a prevailing factor that makes young people vulnerable to recruitment by extremist groups and criminal organisations that promise a sense of purpose and financial gain.

Unequal distribution of wealth

There is no doubt that Nigeria is economically differentiated. While a tiny fraction of the population enjoys immense wealth, most people must constantly struggle to survive (Worimegbe, Powel & Worimegbe, Temitope & Sanjo, Oladimeji 2020). The pattern of wealth distribution and the perception of inequitable wealth distribution often create a sense of injustice and, in turn, the corresponding hatred and resentment. Corruption in government diverts resources away from essential social programmes, further exacerbating poverty and inequality.

The rural-urban divide

In Nigeria, economic opportunities are heavily concentrated in urban centres, leading to a massive rural exodus. This migration puts a strain on urban infrastructure and services, leaving rural communities with limited resources and a weakened sense of security. The lack of effort in development programmes and the lack of economic opportunities in rural areas foster feelings of disempowerment and alienation, leading to widespread insurgency and increased criminal activity. (Le, Thai-Ha & Bui, Manh-Tien & Uddin, Gazi. 2022)

The impact of the oil economy

The dependence of the Nigerian state on oil revenues alone has resulted in a volatile and unstable economy (Oguntoye, Mary & Oguntoye, Adenike. 2021). The upward or downward direction of world crude oil prices can inflict enormous damage on the country's financial structure, as it stifles major projects such as education and job creation (Gylych, J., Ahmad Jibrin, A., Celik, B., & Isik, A. 2022). Similarly, the oil wealth confined to the Niger Delta has triggered ethnic rivalries and conflicts over the distribution of oil money between ethnic groups.

Socioeconomic factors in Nigeria are deeply intertwined and form a complex web that contributes significantly to the insecurity crisis (Ndukwe, James, 2023). Addressing these challenges requires a multifaceted approach that focuses on creating jobs, promoting inclusive economic growth, fighting corruption and ensuring equitable distribution of resources in the country. Only then can Nigeria begin to break the cycle of poverty and insecurity that has afflicted it for far too long.

Political instability and governance problems: A cycle of discontent

Nigeria's delicate security situation cannot be fully understood without considering the country's political instability and the infrastructure and governance issues. Inequalities show that poverty, illiteracy and unjust policies generate a climate of discontent that culminates in violence (Kamta, Noel, Hossein & Jürgen 2020).

A legacy of bad governance

Nigeria's political history is often marred by periods of military rule and is also highly unpredictable. This legacy is mainly responsible for a historical culture of mistrust between the government and its people (Ejitu & Chiemela, 2019). The weakness of existing institutions, as well as the lack of trust and transparency in governance, has had a negative impact on the public's perception of government capacity, which necessarily includes the provision of security as well as food, shelter and water. The result is a sense of despair and contempt for the ruling elite.

The corrosive grip of corruption

The level of corruption in Nigeria is now entrenched and affects all strata of the country's leadership. Most civil servants resolve to siphon off funds personally by diverting them for selfish purposes, such as purchasing cars and other superfluous items, instead of allocating them to vitally essential areas such as education, health systems and infrastructure development. This blatant disregard for public needs leads to public discontent and protests. In addition, corruption within the security services undermines their effectiveness and paves the way for the rise of criminal networks.

The poison of identity politics

The multi-ethnicity that characterises Nigeria is, on the one hand, a peaceful and beneficial compound. Unfortunately, it can also be misused to serve political interests. Politicians often do this by using divisive rhetoric and exaggerating the importance of ethnic and religious groups to attract voters. The disproportionate allocation of resources to certain ethnic groups is, in fact, a major factor in the emergence of identity politics, fuelling inter-community conflicts that end up creating a climate of tension and suspicion.

Competition for scarce resources

The extent of Nigeria's natural resources, particularly the abundant oil in the Niger Delta region, has become more of a problem for the country than a facility for economic growth. Competition for the ownership of these resources between different ethnic groups and regions has led to conflicts that have harmed economic development and led to the continued marginalisation of some communities.

Failure to combat marginalisation

The perception of marginalisation of some ethnic groups is deeply rooted. Due to several factors, most of their communities have historically been excluded from political participation and economic opportunities. The government's failure to address these grievances fuels resentment and support for extremist groups or separatist movements that promise a better future.

The security conundrum

The Nigerian government's response to insecurity has often been heavy-handed and essentially military (Oluyemi, Adisa 2018). Accusations of human rights abuses by communities against security forces have only deepened divisions, leading to a lack of collaboration and intelligence gathering. If programmes and social initiatives that would help address the underlying problems of insecurity are not adequately funded, any military action taken would have only limited operational capacity. It should be noted that political instability and governance problems create fertile ground for insecurity in Nigeria. Weak institutions, corruption and growing ethnic cleavages make the nation vulnerable to violence and extremism. A more sustainable approach to security requires tackling these problems head-on by promoting transparency, accountability and inclusive governance. Only then can Nigeria build a more stable and secure future for all its citizens.

Chapter Five

The Rise of Boko Haram (2009-2014)

In Nigeria today, we bear scars, we bear trauma, we bear deep sorrow today. Our children are still in the forests, in the hands of evil men. But most of them have no names. They are only numbers.

Bishop Matthew Hassan Kukah; Christmas Message 2022

The emergence of Boko Haram: From religious austerity to voracious insurgency

Boko Haram, a name synonymous with terror not only in Nigeria but beyond, did not emerge overnight. Its origins and evolution coincide with socio-political and religious grievances in northern Nigeria.

The insurgent group's horrific actions have cemented its place as a symbol of fear. However, Boko Haram's survival and subsequent transformation into a cruel insurgency is the result of latent discontent in northern Nigeria (Dada, Onyebuchi & Ezeanya 2022). Ethnicity, the policy of marginalisation and a particular conception of religion helped to create the conditions for ideological development. This latent situation of dissatisfaction eventually collapsed, transforming Boko Haram into a religious extremist organisation obsessed with seizing political power in the country.

Annual breakdown of security incidents (2009-2024)

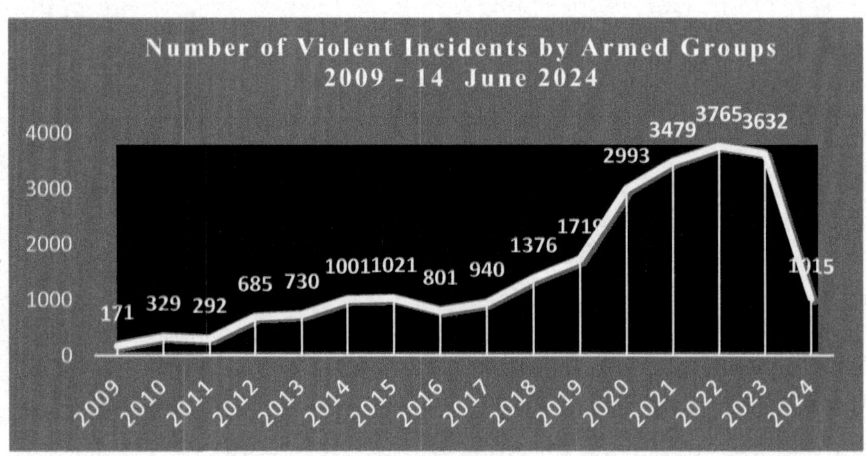

Fig.1. Violent incidents by armed groups 2009-June 14, 2024

The graph above shows the number of violent incidents carried out by different armed groups since 2009, with data extending to June 14, 2024. The period between 2009 and 2014 saw a major increase in reported armed attacks. The upward trend continued beyond 2014 and almost tripled from 1001 to nearly 3000 by the end of 2020. Furthermore, there was a significant increase in the number of violent incidents between 2020 and 2022. The upward trend continued beyond 2022, although the rate of increase levelled off towards 2023 and has seen a noteworthy decrease as of June 2024.

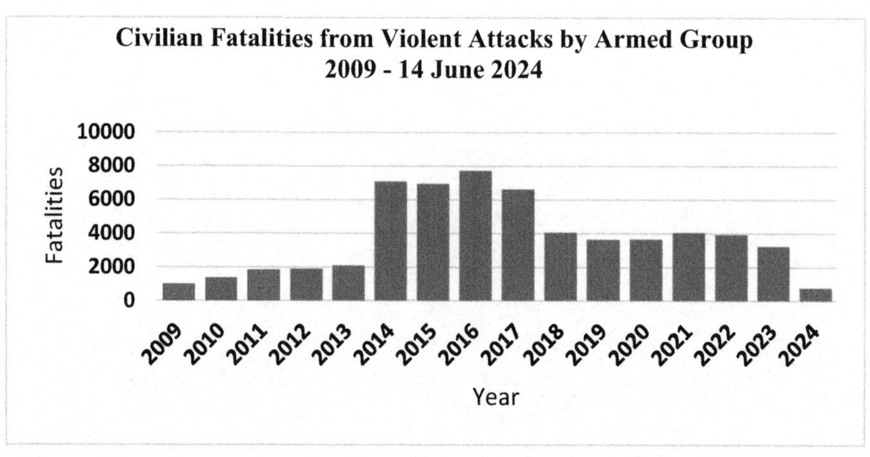

Fig.2. Civilian Fatalities from Violent Attacks 2009- June 14, 2024

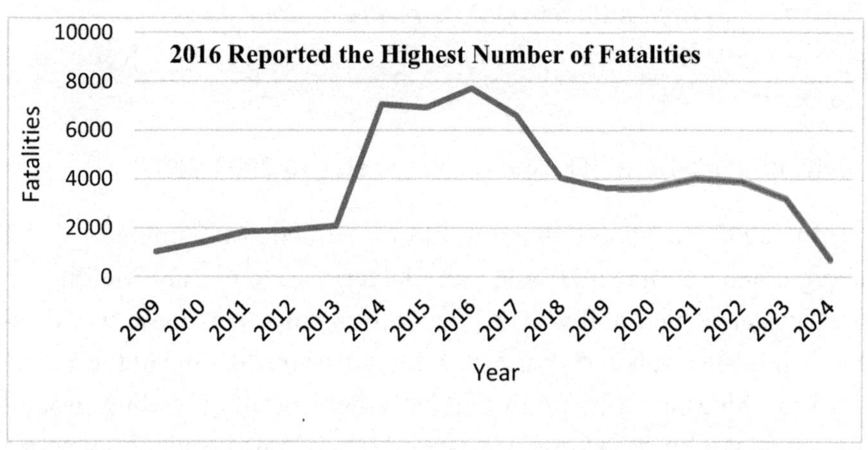

Fig.3. Civilian Fatalities from Violent Attacks 2009- June 14, 2024

According to the data above, the number of civilian fatalities had increased since 2009 and surged dramatically in 2014 through to 2016 which reported the highest fatality figures. However, there has been a sharp decline in reported fatalities since 2017, with 2024 reporting the lowest rates so far. It is noteworthy that Boko Haram was responsible for a significant number of civilian deaths, especially between 2009 and 2014. It is estimated that more than 35,000 people had been killed as a result of Boko Haram attacks between 2009 and 2020. Despite the increase in the activities of armed groups as shown in fig.1. Increased military operations are a major factor responsible for the sharp decline in civilian fatalities seen since 2017 as shown in the graph above.

Seeds of discontent: The early years refer to 2002-2009

In 2002, a then-unknown cleric named Muhammad Yusuf inaugurated a mosque and an Islamic school in Maiduguri, northeastern Nigeria. It was this peer group, known as Jama'at Ahl as-Sunnah lid-Da'wah wa'l-Jihad (also known as the 'People of the Sunna for Preaching and Jihad'), that quickly became the breeding ground for what later became known as Boko Haram. Yusuf's ideology began with a campaign against the introduction of Western ways of thinking, which he believed would lead to the exploitation of the most vulnerable members of society and be replaced by a more puritanical version of Islam. He criticises the Nigerian government for its secularism and the inadequacy of its ethical principles in the light of Islam.

Radicalisation and escalation (2009-2014)

The style of Yusuf's messages and his ability to influence more and more disillusioned young people, particularly those who were unemployed and living in poverty, were gaining ground. The armed response in 2009 marked a turning point in the history of the Islamic community. It was Yusuf's death that led to violent reprisals by his group, giving Boko Haram the impetus to become a fully-fledged warrior sect.

With Abubakar Shekau in the saddle, Boko Haram's ideology is becoming much more jihadist. An insurgent group has launched a campaign of incidents in which it has attacked police stations, government offices and Christian communities. These attacks were triggered by growing dissatisfaction with the Nigerian State, which is seen as both corrupt and un-Islamic. The ultimate aim of the Boko Haram terrorist organisation was to crush the government structure and establish a brutal caliphate based on a rigid interpretation of Sharia law.

2009: Boko Haram launches its first major attack in July, targeting police stations and government buildings in Maiduguri, Borno State. This attack became the first strike of a series of attacks in the northeast part of the country, which was aimed at setting up an Islamic State. The group's ideology, which rejects the Western education system and encourages the implementation of Sharia law, found echoes among the marginalized in the region, thus growing the attraction and support for the group.

2010: To stem the rising acts of violence, the Nigerian government intensifies its hunt for Boko Haram by carrying out security operations in the northeast region. Although this crackdown is progressively giving rise to the so-called reprisal violence and bombings across the land, the Boko Haram militants continue targeting civilians, security forces, and government institutions within the country more deliberately. The ruthless nature of violence in the country, where innocent people become the targets, escalates hatred and mistrust among the population, thereby widening the gaps between different religions and ethnicities.

2011: Boko Haram stages a series of high-profile attacks, including the first attack against a Western interest - the bombing of the United Nations Headquarters in Abuja, which killed 23 people and injured 80 others.

2012: In response to increasing violence, the Nigerian military launches Operation Lafiya Dole as a comprehensive attempt to suppress the group. The mission predictably increases the frequency of fight exchanges between security forces and terrorists, as well as the departure of innocent people from areas that are heavily affected by conflicts. Though the first successive military offensive by the army resulted in promising advances, Boko Haram is still executing assaults and seizing control of the vast regions in northeastern Nigeria.

2013: Boko Haram widens its operations and captures part of the northeast territory of Nigeria, proclaiming the formation of an Islamic State. The group's territorial expansion, which is an additional challenge, makes it difficult for the authorities to stem the tide and restore security in the area. Boko Haram's control over strategic areas enables it to carry out attacks with impunity and exert influence over local communities through intimidation and coercion.

In April 2014, the world witnessed Boko Haram's barbaric escalation of violence with an increase in the kidnapping of women and girls, signalling new frontiers not only in the insurgency but also in evil, in the form of the captivity of large numbers of women and girls. In a daring attack, terrorists stormed a girls' boarding school in the community of Chibok, Borno State, and abducted nearly 300 girls. This horrific incident shook the world and sparked the *#BringBackOurGirls* campaign, calling for the release of the abducted girls. This incident demonstrates that civilians, particularly women and children, are vulnerable to abduction and the deprivation of their rights in conflict-affected regions. International public opinion was deeply shocked by the actions of this group, which abducted children to serve its perverse ideas. The media worldwide covered the case, bringing international attention to the wickedness of this group.

This event marked a turning point. Before this event, Boko Haram, once barely known outside Nigeria, now became the focus of the world's attention. The kidnapping has become a sign of extremism and the eclipse of violence by the group in Nigeria. The international community has realised that the crisis in the region can no longer be ignored. World leaders are speaking out against the kidnappings and pledging to support Nigeria in its fight against terrorism.

The kidnapping triggered a phenomenal campaign on social networks. The hashtag *#BringBackOurGirls* has become the people's sounding board, bridging divides worldwide and calling for the girls' safe return. The girls' struggle has not escaped the public eye, with celebrities, campaigners and ordinary people joining the campaign. Their 'No Abandonment' campaign put pressure on the authorities to act.

Boko Haram's emergence as a global terrorist organisation after Shekau's death has intensified its internal divisions. A breakaway faction emerged - the Islamic State West Africa Province (ISWAP) - and swore obedience to the Islamic State group. The group is still determined to carry out attacks, even though it has suffered setbacks during military operations led by the Nigerian government and the multinational force. This is particularly the case in the northeast country, where the group is active. The group has created an environment of fear and uncertainty with its kidnappings for ransom. This has exacerbated the situation and led to instability in the region.

The Boko Haram insurgency and its escalation represent a powerful combination of social grievance, religious ideology and political instability. Understanding the roots of

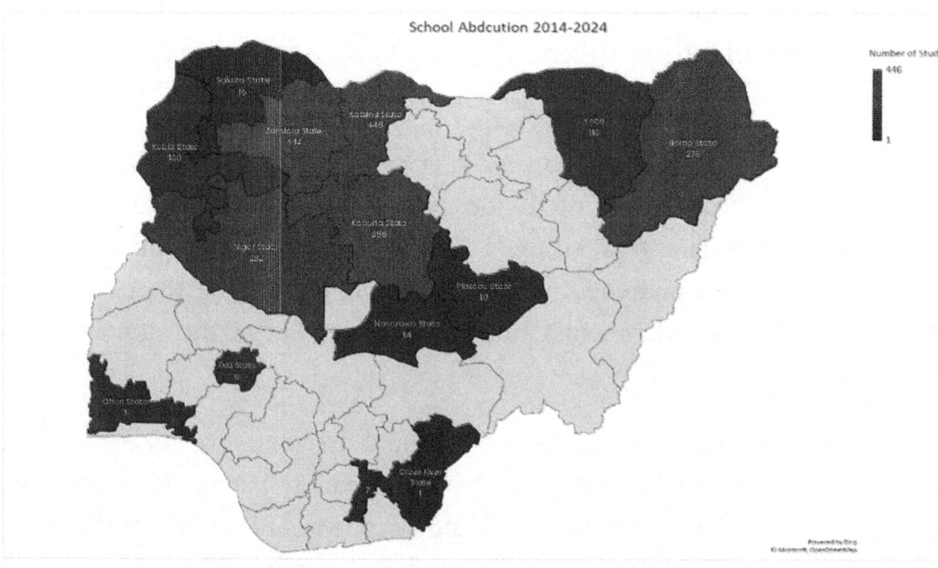

Fig. 4. Number of School Abductions/ State: April 2014 – July 2024

Boko Haram is essential to developing effective strategies to counter its violent extremism and create a more peaceful and secure future for Nigeria.

2015: Muhammadu Buhari won Nigeria's presidential elections as he promised to focus on security and defeat the insurgent group Boko Haram. His regime oversees notable advancement of the Nigerian military, which effectively recaptures the areas lost to Boko Haram's influence and reduces the terrorist group's operational capabilities. Nevertheless, Boko Haram is still persistent and persistently continues to launch sporadic attacks in the northeastern part of the country, especially in remote outskirts and rural areas where security controls and monitoring are minimal.

2016: Another faction of Boko Haram, Islamic State West Africa Province (ISWAP), comes into being, thus making it even more difficult to curb insurgency in the northeast. Unlike Boko Haram, ISWAP resorts to a more hostile and diffused strategy by attacking military bases, villages, and humanitarian aid facilities. While ISWAP illustrates the dynamicity of the insurgency and the obstacles created by splits and rifts inside Boko Haram, many underlying complexities go beyond such superficial appearance and deserve deeper understanding and analysis.

2017: Kidnapping for ransom becomes a money spinner for criminals all over Nigeria as criminal gangs operate in different areas and target both the rich and the poor. The prevalence of kidnappings is directly connected to the deterioration of law and order, which is also characterized by weak law enforcement and loss of communal values. High-profile abductions, including those targeting entire communities and prominent individuals, draw attention to the scale and sophistication of criminal networks involved in the illicit trade.

2018: The Nigerian government launches Operation Safe Corridor, a rehabilitation and reintegration programme targeted at former Boko Haram combatants and other fighters. This programme aims to eradicate the underlying causes of extremism and provide the disengagement from violence through alternative paths. Nevertheless, the scheme's effectiveness in preventing recidivism among participants remains a subject matter of dispute.

2019: The security situation in north-central Nigeria rapidly deteriorates, with what is generally called "herders-farmers clashes," which in actuality are violent attacks on communities, including attempts to forcefully take over ancestral lands, causing multiple fatalities and the displacement of communities. The problem, as compounded by intensifying competition for space, resources, tribalism and ethnicity, highlights the multidimensionality of socioeconomic and environmental issues that contribute to insecurity in Nigeria. The government's strategy to fight the crisis is condemned as being incoherent and ineffective in addressing the problem in the long term.

2020: The COVID-19 pandemic exacerbates Nigeria's security challenges, leading to increased banditry, kidnapping, and communal violence. The pandemic strips people of their livelihoods, test Public Health systems beyond their limits, and amplifies existing inequities, thereby igniting opportunities for criminals to thrive by taking advantage of the prevailing conditions. The Nigerian government's response to the pandemic is handicapped by corruption, mismanagement, and the lack of resources, which erodes the chances of stabilizing insecurity even more.

2021: Despite ongoing military operations and regional cooperation efforts, Boko Haram and ISWAP continue to carry out occasional but deadly attacks in the northeast. Other terrorist groups, especially those that are referred to as bandits by locals, continue to target vulnerable communities, killing dozens, kidnapping scores, and displacing thousands of civilians. Most viciously, these groups aim to kill civilians and force people to move from the area. The persistence of insurgency highlights the deep nature of the security crisis in Nigeria. It shows how difficult it is for efforts to bring about permanent peace and stability in the region. Inter-regional cooperation, intelligence sharing, and targeted counter-insurgency operations are the main pillars to combat the risk posed by terrorist groups.

2022: Insecurity continues to spread nationwide, allowing criminals to exploit vulnerabilities and conduct their attacks brazenly on communities and schools. The proliferation of armed groups and criminal networks symbolizes the failure of governance, corruption, and impunity in Nigeria, while security forces have failed to handle evolving threats appropriately. The failure of the authorities to address the fundamental security issues gives rise to public anger and destroys the faith in state institutions.

2023: The Nigerian government finds itself under increasing pressure to find a solution for insecurity, with demand for reform of the security sector and good governance as part of the solution to eliminate ground causes of violence. The complexity and interrelationship of the same illuminates the concept of comprehensive and inclusive solutions to the security challenge. Efforts to combat insecurity must prioritize addressing underlying grievances, promoting social cohesion, and strengthening institutions to build resilience and ensure sustainable peace and development.

2024: To date, security remains a major concern in Nigeria, with kidnap for ransom and banditry continuing to pose significant challenges to national security and socioeconomic development. The continuance of insecurity clearly indicates that sustained efforts are required to address the root causes of violence, strengthen governance institutions, and promote inclusive development. Building a more resilient and safer Nigeria requires a multifaceted approach to security issues that involves regional cooperation, community engagement, and targeted interventions.

Chapter Six

A Text Announcing My Death

There's a big difference between death threats and love letters - even if the person writing the death threats still claims to actually love you. Of course, considering I once tried to kill someone I loved, maybe I had no right to judge.

Richelle Mead

Strange number: Hello, Father Stephen

Me: How are you?

Strange number: Fr Stephen, I'm fine and you?

Me: I'm fine

Strange number: The network is bad

There's something I want to tell you

Me: Who is it, please?

Strange number: My name is Kelvin. You don't know me. Father Stephen, if I tell you this, you should promise to keep it to yourself.

Me: Kelvin, where is he from, please? What's the problem?

Strange number: It's a matter of life.

Me: What happened?

Strange Number: How much will you pay me to tell you? Let's negotiate the price first if you like

Me: I don't know you. I don't know you. You said you knew me; it's a question of life, and you're talking price. I wish you luck.

Funny number: We're hired to kill you.

Me: By whom?

Still in shock and fear

The text surprised and shocked me. I didn't sleep for two days after the conversation. The text made me agitated. I didn't know what to do; I just sat there for 72 hours. When I regained consciousness, I started to act. I sent the text to my superiors in Abuja, and I sent the text to the bishop, I sent the same text to my close friends inside and outside the country. While writing this book, I asked one of them to check his phone and see if he could still provide me with the text message, I had sent him. That's what he did.

I reported the message to the Nigerian police, the DSS and private security experts. After analysing the text, one of them was convinced that a swindler might want to use me to make money. I felt the same way at the time. But he urged me to be more careful about my personal safety and not take it for granted.

When I spoke to my bishop about it, he wasn't sure what to think either. He thought it could go either way that someone might want you to feel indebted to them for saving their life in this way. However, he encouraged me to take my personal safety more seriously and inform the relevant authorities.

Back at my church, I only told the church council chairman about the incident. I tried not to set off any alarm bells in the community if the alarm was false. And I couldn't bear the dishonour of a false alarm. So, I kept the message confidential, but in all honesty, I was scared for my life.

Chapter Seven

The D-Day

Even though I walk through the valley of the shadow of death, I will fear no evil, for you are with me; your rod and your staff they comfort me. **Psalms 23:4**

Journey through thorns and snake paths

Mai Kambu is generally, a very quiet village, in Katsina State, northwestern part of Nigeria. On this faithful day their peace and serenity, was invaded by the terrorists. On the evening of the 24th May, 2022. We just finished super, had some good laughter on the table, made jokes with each other while on the table, we had our regular night prayers and bid each other good night. This was after the day's hectic activities, which included: early Morning Masses in two communities, long office hours, and visits to some bereaved communities as a result of terrorist attacks. I particularly retired around 11:40pm that day. Not long into my sleep, I had a loud bang and loud sound in my room. The first word I remember hearing was. *Ka tashi kayi baki* (wake up you have visitors). And the kidnappers shouted all the louder *inna fada* (where is Fr)? The shock or confusion of the moment didn't allow me to think straight. I didn't even know what to say. They dragged me into Father Oliver's room and asked him the same question. He, too, answered in silence. While they were trying to find out where the priest was, other kidnappers went to

Ummie's room to wake her up. she was crying uncontrollably. They took Oliver, Ummie and me to the entrance of the presbytery, we found Hassan crying on the floor. We were then led to the gate of the parish house, there we got some few moments of relief, as some people turned on their lights in our direction, and the bandits were forced to wait and made sure the lights coming to their direction was not a threat. While they were waiting for permission from there commander to proceed with us, one of them brought me a pair of trousers and a footwear to put on.

After five minutes, they got everyone out of the house, and we started walking around the back of the house. We walked for 30 minutes and Ummie screamed because of the thorns she stepped on. At that point I removed my footwear and gave it to her. From then on, I started walking without shoes; after an hour's walk, I paused to identify myself. I told them: I AM FATHER, I AM THE PRIEST. They asked me again if I was the priest. I answered in the affirmative. I quickly begged them to release the other three so they could go with me, as it was apparent, they had all come for me. They told me to sit on the ground. At that point, I thought they were going to shoot me. You remember the text message from chapter six, right?

The bandits then asked me: where's the money for the cereals you sold yesterday? I was shocked by this question but a little relieved. I was shocked because I was least expecting it, relieved because I sensed that perhaps they were only after the money. I told them the money was on the table in my room. One of them showed regret by putting both hands on his head. He wanted to take the money, but his commander said they had to continue their journey.

We continued along frightening, challenging paths: rocky, stony, thick agricultural ridges, and muddy. As we went along, the Fulani made sounds as if they were talking to their cows when they came to areas where they suspected a human presence. If the person responded the same way, it meant they were in safe hands. Otherwise, they stopped to let them pass.

We worked for at least two hours. At one point, we stopped, were blindfolded and asked to wait. A car came to collect us and transfer us to another location. I couldn't work out exactly where the car was going. We drove for about 30 minutes, and then the car stopped to drop us off, blindfolded. When we got out, we waited for a while, and suddenly, another haggard-looking man appeared with no clothes or footwear on.

As soon as he arrived, we became the five people abducted that night. We continued our perilous journey towards the unknown destination the bandits were leading us to. They hated any noise or sound coming from us. Even when we felt like coughing, we were scolded or hit at. The difficult journey continued, with me holding Hassan and Ummie's hands from time to time, reassuring them of God's intervention and love. As we continued, I asked Father Oliver to offer prayers of absolution for all of us. I also offered the prayers of absolution. Just in case we didn't make it out alive, we could have the benefit of dying in grace.

The path we took was very rocky and stony, I personally suffered as we went along, partly because I had no footwear on. We walked over sharp stones that tore my toes and foot. The bandits seemed familiar with the paths in the darkest part of the night. We moved without any form of light, but they could clearly see the paths we were taking.

At specific points, the bandits asked us to take off our shirts to avoid any reflection from the lights. They were all wearing black clothes. They were cautious whenever they saw a reflection of light; no matter how far away the lights were, they waited to see who it was. The moment they asked us to take off our shirts was intense because they met a man who shone a light on them for almost ten minutes. In our hearts, we prayed to God to transform these lights into a miracle. We hoped this would be one of those moments when God would intervene even before we reached the bandits' destination. At certain points, they asked us to lie down on the ground to allow the person shining the lights on them from the other end to move.

After waiting about twenty minutes for the lights to go out at the other end, we continued on our way. This time, they had to hasten us up because they had wasted time waiting. They got us moving faster than expected.

The First stop

We went through the forest for the next 3 hours and arrived at a hut around 5 am. The hut looked like a family compound. Before we all entered the hut, they asked us if anyone wanted to urinate because if you enter this 'room,' you won't leave again for anything in the world.

We went into the hut, the fifteen kidnappers and the five of us. The best way to describe these living conditions is 'pit toilet.' The bandits all smoked weed and gave off all sorts of body odours. The stench made many of us nauseous, and we couldn't even vomit if we wanted to. Towards the end of the morning, they brought us some leftover rice that the bandits had eaten. The food was tasteless, but we had to eat to regain strength. After the morning meal, they were kind enough to ask us if we wanted to relieve ourselves. We all said yes. They brought us a bucket to urinate in, which everyone did, but when I was given the bucket to urinate in, I waited almost five minutes, and the urine didn't come out. That's when I started to worry. I knew I'd taken water when we arrived early in the morning. So, I was shocked that the urine didn't come out. My mind was troubled, and even the urine realised my situation.

During our stay, we could hear the noise of children playing, women cooking, pounding; and doing chores. We could also listen to cars and bicycles going by. So apparently it looked like a family compound where the children were living a normal life. From the silence we were forced to maintain in the 'room,' it seemed obvious that the owner(s) of the house didn't want the children and perhaps the women of the house to know about their father's type of activity (though I doubt they really didn't).

Crossing the water

In the middle of the night, after endless hours of walking without the moon's light. The bandits drew our attention to the fact that there was a river ahead of us in an hour. I imagined the torchlight existing only in their eyes. About an hour after the announcement, they asked us to hold hands to enter and cross the river. Personally, I have a deep-seated phobia for water, and I'm pretty sure everyone of us there except the bandits does. But at that moment, it was between life and death. I gathered my courage and held Ummie and Father Oliver's hands, Hassan held the bandits' hands and Father Oliver at the other end. As we crossed, the volume of water kept increasing. It wasn't very comforting. The water engulfed Ummie, and I had to carry her on my back, probably because I was up to my neck in water. I prayed that we wouldn't fall and that I wouldn't lose my balance. Crossing the water was one of the most frightening parts of this horrible journey. At that point, Psalm 23 was powerful and very real to me as I crossed the water. I prayed hard not to fall into the water because none of us carried any live jackets, and none knew how to swim. Any fall in that river would have certainly resulted in deaths.

The second round of trekking

Around 6 p.m., we were brought the second meal before continuing our journey. It was *tuwo da miyan kuka*. This is a common local dish in northern Nigeria. However, this type of dish was very poorly prepared. There was nothing in the food to stimulate our appetite. We showed signs of refusing to eat any more, the bandits retorted, you'd better eat, or you'll all starve to death on the road. At this point, we had to encourage each other to eat as much as our taste buds would allow. After the meal, they ushered us out of the 'room' around 7 pm to begin a new series of walk. We moved around for a while and waited under a tree for someone they had apparently sent to bring them some fried yams. We sat on the ground, waiting for the man. He arrived in no time and gave them yams in nylon and gave us a few meagre pieces of yam. Whenever we showed signs of dissatisfaction with their meals, they simply added: you'll starve if you don't eat what we give you. A statement I quickly understood. All the other food we eat comes with a few drops of water, but the yam we ate had none. When we tried to ask for water, one of the kidnappers insulted us.

We continued our walk toward this unknown destination in silence, and haste. We were insulted or beaten as soon as we showed signs of fatigue or weakness. So, we constantly had to work fast to avoid being run over or insulted. On several occasions, we fell into ditches and pits and bumped into thorny sticks. Each time we fell, the bandits insulted us for falling into a ditch or pit because of a route we had never followed. Several hours into our trek, I was exhausted. Ummie was panting heavily and struggling to keep up, but the sight of the bandits with their rifles meant that none of us could think of stopping. I saw Father Oliver, Hassan and the other man they all looked fitter and more robust. However, I knew they had no strength left; it was the fear of death that kept them going.

I tried to communicate with the rest of us to implore the bandits to let us rest for at least five minutes, but they were all afraid to make such a request. We kept going, but I couldn't keep up with the speed and energy, so I collapsed to create some rest for myself and the others. The bandits shouted at me to get up, or they'd kill me. As I was weak, they hung up their guns to fire, but Ummie and Hassan's moans woke me up. I didn't have the strength to continue but I had to pick up the courage to move on.

As I said earlier, the bandits were constantly smoking weed. When I felt I needed something to help me regain my strength, I asked them to give me some weed to smoke; they told me; that would be too strong for me but that they would give me some drugs to swallow. Instead, they gave Ummie and me two tablets of tramadol each. We took the tablets with some water we found along the way. It looked like stagnant water. The medication weakened me in every sense of the word. The little strength I had disappeared completely; I couldn't even move my legs. It was Hassan Fareed, who carried me on his shoulder to continue the journey. I started to run out of breath and became very thirsty. I shouted for water and called the bandits. One of them approached me gently and said: 'Fada, be strong. We'll soon reach a place where there's water.'

We arrived at a well; the bandits had to take a break to revive me; with water and milk, which I later learned had been taken from my fridge in the house after they took us, they stole food, drinks, tins of milk, phones, laptops, money and anything else of value. After regaining our strength to continue, we came to a mango tree and they asked us to pick mangoes and eat them. We all stopped to pick the mangoes and eat them. We picked the mangoes off the ground and ate them. No one thought to clean their hands. As I ate the mangoes that evening, I saw myself living like a grazing animal, eating everything I saw on the ground. In the silence of my heart, I whispered: 'Stephen, you see what Nigeria has made of you: an animal.'

We continued this terrible journey until morning hours. As we approached, we saw powerful lights, which looked like industrial lamps used by large companies. The lights kept moving and shining. Some of the bandits told us that these lights were our destination. Personally, I felt happy, thinking that at least our final destination was a place where we could see light. And a bright one at that.

Off with the bikes

As we approached the lights, I saw people standing by each light and heard the sound of some motorbike with an engine. In fact, they were motorbikes waiting to take us to another destination. People were waiting for us to arrive. There were about ten motorbikes, so they put us in pairs on each motorbike; three of us were on each. The captives were in the middle; the bandits were two per motorbike. I asked the man on my motorbike how many hours we had left to reach our destination. He replied that we would arrive in the next 45 minutes. To make sure that the bandit on my bike was also accessible, I asked him: 'Please, can I have some Sprite? Can I have a soda when we get there? He quickly replied in the affirmative. The question I asked him will be addressed when I talk about life in the camp in later chapters.

The motorbike journey took between 2 and 3 hours. While on the motorbike, I was sleeping because of tiredness; Father Oliver's motorbike was close to mine. At least I counted three times I saw them fall off the motorbike very badly. Each time they fell, the bandits insulted him, shouted at him and hit him for his fall. At one point, I felt sick when I saw Father Oliver fall, his trousers tearing instantly.

We finally arrived at our destination late in the morning.

Chapter Eight

Daily Life with The Kidnappers

"Alone in my prison cell I continued to be tormented by the fact that I was 48 years old in the prime of my life, that I had worked for eight years as a bishop and gained so much pastoral experience and there I was isolated, inactive and far from my people"

Francis Xavier Nguyen Van Thuan, 2021

This chapter is the main thesis of our 31-day experience. The horror, humiliation, flogging and pain occurred during those days. The ones we experienced on arrival were very bad. However, we will certainly run out of words to describe what we experienced here. The bandits who took us from our homes entrusted us to other bandits to look after us. A man in his twenties called, *Uban Slow*, ran the camp where we were kept.

As soon as we arrived, I was in a hurry and asked where I could go to relieve myself. I looked at him, and he insulted me. Moreover, he told me I was never to look at him again. He hit me and insulted me again. In my usual playful attitude, not realising where I was, I smiled and asked him nicely and playfully: Why are you insulting and hitting me? When I had finished using the toilet and entered the hut where they were guarding us, the guards called me over and said: 'So I had the courage to defy them and ask them questions, right?'

They told me to lie down on the ground and I was whipped mercilessly. After a few strokes with the stick, they let me go back to the hut, in pains. As soon as we had 'settled in' to our new home. We tried to look at the four other victims in the hut; they were four men from the ECWA Gidan Garba church. A pastor and three of his members. They had been abducted nine days before we arrived. We couldn't greet each other usually like human beings, we could only see each other in pain and greet each other with tear-filled eyes. When he found out I was a Catholic priest, Yunusa, one of the young men from the Ecwa church, said to me: 'I'm so sorry, fada, I'm so sorry. I'm so sorry, fada, I'm so happy to meet you finally, but very sad to meet you here in this state.' I replied that it was God's will.

We were having a quiet chat when one of the bandits guarding us asked in Hausa: *Zaku sha shayi* (would you like some tea?). All those who had just arrived that morning answered unanimously in the affirmative. Yunusa and his brothers put their hands to their heads in shock and disbelief. We never knew what this question meant. The bandits came into the hut with canes, sticks and anything that could hurt us and started whipping us and making us cry. They whipped us so badly. They made everyone in the hut cry with so much pains. The more we cried out and shouted Jesus, the more they whipped us. We had to learn to endure the pain of the scourging without shouting the name of Jesus. However, I personally cried out to Jesus in my heart at each blow of the stick or cane that touched me.

This exercise lasted at least thirty minutes. When they finished, we had no life left in us. We wanted to lie on the ground. They ordered us to face the wall. Our backs were positioned so we could be flogged again each time they wanted to continue. During the flogging, they ceased all our sacramentals and medals. *Uban Slow* (the bandits' leader guarding us) started wearing the rosary he had ceased from Ummie Hassan. He wore the finger rosary the whole time we stayed with them in the bush.

At the end of the evening. They brought us the first round of food. It was rice and beans cooked only with palm oil. This was our only food for the next 31 days. What's more, this is what Yunusa and his three colleagues from the ECWA church ate nine days before our arrival. They brought the food in a stainless-steel bowl so we could all eat. They asked Ummie to eat first before giving us the rest. This is how we ate for the next 31 days. We all ate with our hands, and very often, we ate without washing our hands. When we finished eating, the water they brought us to drink was brown and muddy. But we drank it with great pleasure. At first, I wondered what I would do with such water. But the rest is history because it was the only choice of water. I wasn't drinking enough, in my mind, so as not to damage my system. But not drinking enough muddy water was another problem in itself. I started having difficulty breathing, and I felt in my body that I was running out of water. So, I started drinking enough dirty, muddy water.

We all gathered around the plate of rice and beans, and after three minutes, the plate was empty, and we were still starving. But we had nothing left to eat for the day.

The first visit and the calls

We were captured on Tuesday evening and arrived at our destination Thursday morning. The first time we were able to talk to our family was around late morning of Friday. The person in charge of negotiations arrived with five heavily armed men. They took us out of the hut and ordered us to sit on the ground. We just sat there; our faces turned towards the ground. They started laughing at each of us and insulting us. They threatened to kill us if our people didn't comply with their demands. They first tried to establish a link between the four of us and wanted to negotiate our freedoms individually.

They asked for the identity of Ummie and Hassan, and I told them they were my nieces, their mother being my eldest sister.

Consequently, any negotiations concerning them had to be addressed to me. They asked for the identity of Father Oliver Okpara, and I told them that Oliver was my cook and driver and that he ran errands for me in the parish. In this way, the whole negotiation rested on me alone.

So, the bandits started asking for 150 million ransoms to get the four of us out. They asked me if I understood their request, and I said yes. If we call you and you say anything less, we'll kill you,' I said yes, sir.

They then asked me who they were going to talk to, and I asked Malam Oliver (not referring to him again as Fr Oliver) to get Father Habila Samaila's number from his phone and give it to them. He got the number and gave it to their boss in other to call Father Habila. They gave me the phone to call him immediately, and I said, 'Fr Habila, it's me, Fr Stephen. I'm here with Malam Oliver, Ummie and Hassan. I told him we weren't happy there and that they should do everything possible to get us out. Through him, I also appealed to the people of Gidan Mai Kambu to come to our rescue. I told him. 'The bandits are asking for 150 million Naira ($1.500,000). Please, he should try to get them that money'. I ended my appeal and handover the phone to the bandits. We were extremely happy to hear from Fr Habila.

Shocks about my data from the bandits

When the bandits came to see us after our arrival, they started by questioning us one by one. They asked Ummie for her contact details. They asked her how much money she could raise. Could she give them 50 million? They asked Hassan, her brother, and Father Oliver the same question. When they came to see me, I had to connect all three of them to me. I told them that Father Oliver was my driver and a cook, he had nothing, and that Ummie and Hassan were my nephew and niece. Furthermore, their mother, who was my eldest sister, was very ill (holy lie). On this basis, I told them that I was the only person they should contact to obtain their ransom.

The bandits asked how much they could get from me because I was rich. I have good connections. They told me that they had heard that I travelled to the United States every fortnight. I came back from America a week before they picked me up. They said I had a lot of money. I had travelled to many parts of the world, and I could never have travelled to all those countries if I didn't have money. They told me I had travelled to Italy, Malaysia, Austria, England, etc. I tried to explain to them that I didn't have any money. I tried to explain to them that these trips are not self-financed and that the Church finances them. They also told me that the federal government pays me N750,000 ($3000) a month. I was on the federal government payroll because I had many connections with the government.

Insults from the bandits

The bandits seized every opportunity to insult us; their lips were wet with all sorts of insults every day. In one day, they insulted us hundreds of times; What's more, anything can trigger these insults. Whether you say hello or they call your name when you reply, the next word out of their mouth is *Ubanka* (male) *or Ubanki* (Female) depending on who they are insulting. Literally it means your father. But that insult is understood as 'you're stupid.' We had to deal with this daily. Other times, they told us we smelled bad and shouldn't go near them.

The drama between Hassan, Ummie and the Praying Bandits

Hassan and Ummie are siblings. Hassan is a Muslim, while Ummie is a Christian, and she calls him Daddy because he bears the name of their father. It is common in Nigeria for a child to be named after the father and be called Junior or Daddy. As a Muslim, the bandits always called Hassan to pray with them. One of the very notorious kidnappers would always tell Hassan to come out to perform ablution and pray, and he ensured that Hassan prayed five times daily. "It was very surprising when I saw him also observing the daily prayers. I just couldn't help but keep wondering. In fact, I didn't even know what to think."

As a courageous man Hassan would always think of escaping. Ummie would always remind him of what the repercussions may be. 'You know if you do that, you are endangering our lives all,' she'd tell him.

There was a day they woke Hassan up around 5 am to get water. Hassan said: "I got to know the time well. I heard the call of Fajr prayer from a distance, and I summoned the courage to ask one of the kidnappers, and he told me that what the time was. While we were coming back from the lake where we went to get the muddy water, I almost collapsed because the gallon I was carrying was weighing me down, not because I couldn't carry it, but because I had no interest in carrying it, I wasn't doing it with happiness I was being compelled to do what I didn't want to do. At an odd hour, the thought of escaping crept into my head, but what would become of my partners? The level of security given might just increase, or they might even eliminate them, and I might not end up getting out of the forest alive or probably fall into the den of some other horrible kidnappers. Moreover, my kid sister kept ringing it in my ears never to attempt running away."

On another day, while getting the firewood, he got bitten by different insects and scorpions but had no right to complain. If not, he would receive the scolding of his life. He also had to get the firewood because our so-called meals depended on that. Being the kind man, he is, he didn't want to increase our starvation by not getting them. Getting firewood became more adventurous for Hassan because he brought a fruit called Doruwa, which he sometimes brings back to the hut. Some days that would be our only meal for the day, and we all will devour like hungry lions. One day, Ummie grabbed Hassan's hand and gently, with tears in her eyes, said, "Daddy, be careful, okay?

Don't forget to get us doruwa (local fruits) when coming back, and always remember I love you, and we all will be free someday by God's grace," Hassan smiled back at her and assured her he would be careful. We all knew what she meant. Don't think of running away, please.

Death threats

This topic is about the death threats we have received. I've chosen to talk about death threats because there's no better way to explain the reality grammatically. They have indeed killed several people in the camp, and they will continue to kill, so the threats are not empty. They were honest, palpable, emotional and saddening.

When we arrived, they told us that they were serious about all their demands and that if they weren't met, the only option they had was to kill. They told us about a pastor who had been shot in the leg and left here to rot. I later confirmed that he was Father Felix, from the Catholic Diocese of Zaria.

Every day, the bandits reminded us of how useless our corpses would be when they killed us and hand us over to the vultures in the bush. The first day we arrived, they told us to look over there - that's where they kill people and leave them so that their rotting bodies don't smell. They told us: 'If you have any doubts, we'll go and show you, but you can be sure that once we've shown you, we won't let you come back to tell the story.'

For me, the biggest death threat I ever received was when they arrived in the third week and told me that our people weren't serious about their negotiations, so I had to tell them who I was prepared to give up to be killed so that the people who were negotiating with them would know that they were serious. They came to me in the morning to tell me that. I looked at them up and down and said, I'll give myself up. They asked me if I was sure of what I'd just said, I said yes.

In the evening, they came to tell me that it was time. I got up, said goodbye to everyone in the camp and left. I left them in tears and agony while the bandits put me in front with their guns behind. We walked a few metres away, and one of the bandits called out to me loudly: Fada!!!! *Ka Koma*. Which means Father, go back. Honestly, I didn't believe it was real. All I was waiting for was a gunshot.

I turned around and went back to our little cabin. When I entered, everyone inside was crying their eyes out. They were more than relieved to see me back.

Living with wild animals

For us, life in the bush was like a departure into the Hobbesian state of nature. Man, and animal lived side by side. From the moment they took us at Gidan Mai Kambu to the forest where we were kept at Birnin Gwari, we became friends with reptiles and dangerous animals. We lived in the forest for the number of days we were there. We came in contact with snakes, scorpions and dangerous insects whose names we didn't know. Most of us knew that mosquitoes were dangerous insects to avoid. But we suddenly realised mosquitoes were much nicer insects than the ones that bit us. When we arrived, Yunusa and Yusif's pores were bloody from the unknown insects that had bitten them. These same dangerous insects made us all bleed with every bite.

One day, we begged the bandits to use insecticides to reduce the number of insects in the hut. It was a very unwise request, which almost cost us our lives that day because, during the night, scorpions stung some of us in sensitive places on our bodies - our heads, our chests and some of our legs. Forest snakes hissed constantly. A large frog used to come and spend the night with us. The frog goes out in the morning and comes back in the evening. And if you have a good sense of the ecosystem, snakes are not far away wherever there are frogs. We waited for the frog to return one day, but it never did. We sensed that it may have been eaten by snake.

Cooking

One of the first questions the bandits asked Ummie as soon as we arrived was: *"Ummie, Kin iya da fa abinci?"* (Ummie, can you cook?) She quickly replied NO. They were taken by surprise and wondered what nonsense the young lady was saying. Overhearing this conversation, I quickly whispered to her: if someone asks you why you can't cook, just tell them you have epilepsy. A person with epilepsy doesn't go near water or fire. It was as if we'd beaten them to it. After a few minutes, they returned to Ummie, but why can't you cook? I've had epilepsy since childhood", she replied. Surprisingly, this warmed their hearts. They said, 'What a beautiful young woman, you mean you can't cook? I'm so sorry. How are you going to cook for your husband when you're married? I'll get a housekeeper", Ummie replied.

For me, that answer was simply divine. It was impossible to imagine what would happen to Ummie if she started cooking for them. So, we didn't want to risk such a relationship. Thank goodness the 'lie' worked. For the first two weeks, Hassan Farid, Yunusa and Iliya were the three men the bandits always used to fetch wood in the bush. They would get up very early, to fetch water from the stream or wood for cooking.

The bandits would cook for us, serving us beans, rice, palm oil and seasoning. We ate this food for 31 days. They took turns cooking for us. The five of them who looked after us had different days to cook. One of them in particular was terrible. We hated to watch him cook because he does not clean the pot, he'd used the day before to cook properly, and he certainly didn't clean the plate he used in serving us food either. We were already dirty and stinking, but adding a dirty pot and plate was nauseating.

Music, the lifeblood of the bandits

This is one of the most interesting aspects of staying in the bush. The bandits lived with Music for 24 hours, and their world was noisy. All five of them usually listened to music on their phones at the same time. All five phones are set to the highest volume. When we first noticed this, we thought it was a mistake, but gradually, we discovered this was their habit. They played all kinds of music: hip-pop, gospel, Igbo, Hausa, wedding songs, Arabic and so on. All sorts of songs were played from their phones because they had all kinds of stolen memory cards.

Their music kept us going for a good part of the day, as there were times when very powerful and comforting music was played from their stolen memory cards. We'll never forget Pentecost Sunday that year. It was the first Sunday of our capture. We all woke up to a powerful song by Don Moen about the power of the Holy Spirit, and the three other songs that played afterward were about the power of the Holy Spirit. There was no better assurance from God than those songs the bandits played for us.

Military helicopters

For several days, we saw military helicopters coming into the bush. Sometimes, when the helicopters flew by, the bandits would take cover; sometimes, they would accuse me of having something to do with the presence of these helicopters.

One day, the helicopters started firing at point-blank range. Only God knows whether they were aiming at random or specific targets. As far as we were concerned, we were all lying on the ground with our legs chained together. We couldn't think about taking cover in case the shots were aimed at us.

The shots coming from the sky were more than terrible. We all saw the bandits taking cover and getting into fighting positions.

Boys with guns and weeds

There are a lot of surprises as we lived with the bandits. The first shock I had was the age range of the boys, holding guns and commanding us. They were boys in their teens and twenties. 90% of those we saw were teens and those in their early twenties. In the camp where they kept us, it was a young minor who was supplying weed and cigarettes to his fellow bandits.

Supplying such items also meant that the boy was highly specialised in smoking the weed himself. The boy was also very good at holding weapons and trying to make them, ready for action. The boy who supplied the cigarettes wasn't part of the gang guarding us. But apparently, he was more vicious than the five bandits on our guard. Whenever he appeared, he looked at us with great anger as if he needed a whip to teach us a lesson. One day, I looked at him straight in the eye and refused to bow my head. He looked at me angrily as if to tell me to bow my head. I deliberately refused to take my eyes off him and I said in my heart; Let the worst happen today.

The boy went over to his elders, speaking in Fulfulde and pointing at us. I knew he was denouncing me and some of us who had dared to look him in the eye.

Prayers in the camp

It's almost impossible to describe the level of spirituality we all reached as captives between life and death. Our prayers began the moment we were taken from Gidan Mai Kambu. At first, I was praying and singing loudly when the bandits led us out of the house and ordered us to sit on the ground until the road was clear and we could start moving. A serious hit with the cutlass silenced me. The bandit who was holding me hit me with the knife and said: 'One more word of prayer or song from me, and I'll use this knife to help you finish praying to heaven.'

I had no choice but to continue praying silently in my heart. During the more than twenty hours of the walk, the Hail Mary, filled with grace, never left my lips. Along the way, I remember cognitively celebrating Holy Mass. We began with confessions and a general absolution between Father Oliver and myself. The idea was to prepare ourselves spiritually for the uncertainty ahead. It could mean life or death. Walking towards the bush, we used powerful psalms like Psalm 23 to travel with us. A Psalm we recited three times a day—morning, afternoon and evening.

We all prayed individually and collectively as a group. We prayed fervently because prayer from the heart was all we had left to wield in the world. Prayer was our greatest weapon of encouragement and hope. Thanks to prayer, our hearts were always at peace. We knew we were in a difficult situation, but prayer enabled us to see beyond our current situation. I remember telling Ummie that the most challenging thing God has in store for us is what we're going through. This phase of the journey is the hardest, but be rest assured that the other phases of our lives will be more glorious and deeply rewarding. I spoke as if I were sure of tomorrow (Because he lives, I can face tomorrow) was our constant song. A song that gave us hope even when we had no reason to have any.

As soon as I woke up, I celebrated Holy Mass cognitively. Of course, the sacred species were absent, but in my heart, I felt the power of the Eucharist even without their physical appearance. Celebrating the Eucharist in this way gave me a better understanding of the nature of the Eucharist. It is truly a spiritual nourishment and a profound mystery to contemplate. On the 9th anniversary of my priestly ordination. I woke up with chains on my legs, just like every other day. The chains made me cry and sob softly as I began Mass, and I felt tears welling up in my eyes as I remembered the first day, I wore my ordination chasuble. As I was the only one awake that early morning, I had the opportunity to purify my life that morning by shedding more tears as I once did on the day of my ordination. At the end of my personal prayers, we always prayed together as a group. Holding hands, we silently prayed for so many intentions. We prayed for our situation. We prayed for the Bishop of Sokoto, Matthew Hassan Kukah because we knew that the weight of these problems would fall on his head. We prayed for the Missionary Society of St Paul. Because I once told them that I knew that all the MSPs in the world would mention our names in all their chapels. And I was right. The whole MSP family from all over the world united in prayer for our safe release. We also prayed for our respective families. We knew they would be in great difficulty, and we prayed fervently that God would keep them alive for us, too. We also prayed for my sister, Mary Anne, who was preparing for surgery prior to the abduction.

Freedom in sight

After 30 days in captivity, they came early in the morning to say that our ransom had been paid and that the four of us had to come and prove to Father Habila, the chief negotiator, that we were all alive before he would hand over the money. By this time, Ummie was already losing consciousness; she wasn't talking, and I could literally see her fading away. Father Oliver was weakening, too, as his peptic ulcer had persisted, and Hassan was also very ill, complaining of persistent headaches. Strangely enough, I was the only one un-sick and strong. I was coordinating them all. For my part, I was impatient for us all to be free again. I was also afraid that they wouldn't keep their promises. I was in tears, waiting for freedom and praying calmly. Suddenly, one of them looked at me and asked an eternal question: ‘Can you still forgive us after all we've done to you? I didn't need to think about it and quickly answered: Yes. That, yes really changed my bitter feelings. I instantly felt at peace. And ready to move forward with hope.

A few minutes later, two motorbikes carrying four men arrived and asked where Malam Oliver was. He came forward, and they asked where Ummie was; she came forward and asked them both to get on the motorbikes; they stood between two men each. They told Hassan and myself to stay and that they would come back for us.

At this point, I'm almost sure my blood pressure would be reading 1000/2000. The fear that was gripping me was incredible. Where were they taking Oliver and Ummie to? After confirming that all four of us were alive, they took two and left two. No explanation was given. It was a challenging moment. After an hour spent watching the path that took Ummie and Oliver, *Uban Slow*, the captain of the bandits who was in charge of us, asked me to come so that he could put the chains back on our legs. Hassan and I sat on the ground and he put the chains back on. I looked at Hassan and his state of health, wept silently and prayed for him. I encouraged him to be strong. I told him that very soon, they would come back for us; as they had promised. Later that evening, one of the bandits told me they hadn't released the four of us because they asked for bikes and didn't get any, so we're being held here until they get the four bikes they asked for.

New Arrival

They brought a new arrival into the camp two days before we left at around 4 am. A highly respected man in the community. Alhaji Sanusi. He arrived with a broken ankle as a result of the terrible blows he received from the bandits as they captured him. Alhaji Sanusi came thinking he would leave the next day. The bandits always take their time once they are in this forest because they know that the State would not be looking for anyone near where they were. His arrival was a mixture of pity, fear and hope. Pity because he had broken his ankle and could no longer walk, so he had to get down on his knees to go to the toilet. He was in pain. Intense pain. Fear, because his arrival meant they were still very active and many more would be arriving. Hope, because it meant that some of us would soon be released and others would be taken and replaced there. Clearly, this camp had not been short of victims for many years.

The short time we spent with Alhaji Sanusi was refreshing. We asked him questions about our home, relatives, friends, and the country's politics. He gave us the latest news. And all I could say was that things were still as bad as ever. Things were still as bad as they were before we were kidnapped. Alhaji Sanusi told us briefly how the kidnappers had followed him for three years; every time they came to his house, they returned without success until the last time. He told us how he fought against fifteen armed boys. He fought with his bare hands. He said that the bandits had no strength other than the weapons they were holding. One blow was enough to disarm them, and he fled the house. One of them, who was waiting at the door, aimed at his ankle and hit it with a big stick, and that's how he broke his ankle. They dragged him halfway through the bush. They stopped to give him a special caning session. They beat him and nearly killed him. Fortunately, he too is alive. Quietly nursing his wounds and healing like most of us.

Day 33

It was a Sunday morning, and the day began with heavy rain. The bandits told us to get ready. Hassan and I were going home. At the time, I didn't know what to believe after what had happened three days earlier. I wasn't excited or sad; I was just waiting to see what would happen. At around 2 pm, two motorbikes came to pick us up. Hassan and I were on both bikes between two bandits.

Before leaving, I turned to Yunusa, Yusuf, Iliya and Sanusi, who had become our family. I said a short prayer and wished them freedom one day, too. Yusuf, Iliya and Yunusa were there two weeks before we arrived, and after 33 days, we left them there because their ransom had not been paid.

On the way back. The bandit who was driving the motorbike said to me. *Fada kana da sa'a*. (Fr you are a lucky man.) I asked him why did he say that. He said: because we were asked to collect ransom from you and kill you anyway.' I asked him so what had happened. Why have you not killed me, He replied: 'Every time we talked about your death, we never came to a conclusion".

They took us to where the person who had brought the four bikes came to deliver them, and that person brought us back. He was my parishioner from Gidan Mai Kambu. He was brave enough to have dared to deliver those bikes to them. We arrived in Funtua at around 6 pm, surrounded by family and friends. The two people who caught my eye were my mother, who was waiting for me with her rosary in her hand. Then there was my sister, who was ill and had to have an operation on her hips. My mother was full of confidence and praise when she saw me. Her dry face helped to hold back my tears. Then I quickly asked my sister: 'How did the operation go? This is because it was the last thing on my table before I left 33 days ago. I can't even talk about how happy people were when they saw us. I can only talk about the tears.

Chapter Nine

Phone Calls

When Insecurity Persists beyond 24 hours the State is involved

General Sani Abacha

After our two-day journey, our arrival and our long stay with the kidnappers. This chapter is courtesy of the great man Father Habila Samaila, who helped to retained recorded conversations with the bandits. When they first came to meet us and asked to speak to our people, I personally made sure that the only option open to them was Father Habila Samaila, a very dynamic young priest who helped negotiate and free Monsignor Keke when he was kidnapped in 2021. Father Habila's voice was more than gold to us, even if we could only hear it for five seconds, it gave us energy and life to carry on living in the midst of death and grief. These are the communication channels between our negotiator and the Bandits. A challenge for our security agents in Nigeria.

First records (minutes)

Exchange of pleasantries

Negotiator: how are my people?

Bandit: they are fine

Negotiator: I have told you, the people you've held captive their relatives don't have such an amount.

Bandit: and so, what?

Negotiator: honestly speaking, I don't want us to waste time with this negotiation, just try and consider what I told you initially.

Bandit: now listen to me carefully, the amount I told you is what we want, we cannot go back on it am not going back on it.

Negotiator: please I need you to consider me.

Bandit: I cannot consider you on anything, if you had complied to bring the amount I told you yesterday, I would have released your people by now

Negotiator: you know you are the captain in this boat, that is why am pleading with you

Bandit: so, what do you want me to do for you now?

Negotiator: I have told you already this people are not financially buoyant they are missionaries, who came to help the villagers.

Bandit: and so, what? I have told you I can't help you, it's that amount or nothing.

Second audio (3:13 minutes)

Negotiator: am still pleading with you, please help us.

Bandit: what do you mean by that? What do you want me to do? I am sick and tired of you pestering me always. If you are prepared to have your people back then drop the amount I told you, if you are not ready, I have lot things ahead of me. I don't have time to waste with you.

Negotiator: I have told you those people came for missionary work; they are not as wealthy as you think

Bandit: then that means you are not ready to have them back. If you are ready, you bring the money.

Negotiator: we are more than prepared to have those people back, just try and help us.

Bandit: then what rubbish are you vomiting from your mouth, I won't listen to you anymore. Just go straight to the point and say what I want to hear.

Negotiator: okay we are ready to offer you 1 million.

Bandit: 1 million Naira?

Negotiator: yes

Bandit: but do you know that you are a senseless human being.

Negotiator: I don't understand, why did you say that?

Bandit: now listen to me, if you see even one among then thank God. Take this from me, I will kill all of them and that's a promise. Since I have realized that you are a senseless human being.

You are offering me a million Naira because I have been trying as much as possible to be nice with you; but you want to take it for granted, if you think you're dealing with amateur thieves or bandits then you need to reset the nuts in your head. I am not like them; you are very stupid both you and your one million Naira; to hell with you all.

Negotiator: listen to me; we can negotiate we don't need to quarrel over this.

Bandit: you are a fool, and idiot for that matter, if you called me to tell me about one million, then to hell with you. If you ever call me to tell me about offering 1 million Naira, I'll kill one amongst them and Fr. will be the one to confirm that one of them have been killed.

Negotiator: listen to me please, this is not something we should disagree over, just calm down let's talk.

Bandit: you are nothing but a fool, because you are not the one in their shoes that is why you are talking of offering me a million Naira.

Negotiator: am so sorry, but what I want you to understand is that, we don't have such an amount.

Negotiator (1:44 minutes)

Exchange of pleasantries

Negotiator: so, what is the headway now?

Bandit: how do you mean? What kind of question is that?

Negotiator: what I mean is that we didn’t finalize yesterday.

Bandit: so, what do you what me to tell you? What do you want us to finalize on?

Negotiator: just tell me something consoling that will give me peace of mind.

Bandit: that one is left to you. No matter how cunning you think you want to be you will not succeed, it will never work on me.

Negotiator: am not trying to be cunning.

Bandit: this has fallen upon you all, so just try and take it in good fate; pay the money for the release of your loved ones. If you are not ready then that's none of my business.

Negotiator: am more than prepared. And you can see the signs.

Bandit: you are not at all because I can't see it in you, if you were, you won't be telling me of giving me 1 million.

Negotiator: you know I have tried my best.

Bandit: oh, so you are deceiving yourself with 1 million? Okay keep deceiving yourself that's none of my business.

Fifth recording (5:27 minutes)

Bandit: I can hear you, speak.

Negotiator: please try and reason with me, honestly, I have tried.

Bandit: how do you mean I should reason with you?

Negotiator: I don't like it when you speak in harsh tunes, I don't even like hearing you speak in an angry manner.

Bandit: now listen to me, I swear to God I will deal with you in a way you least expected, I told you about one hundred and fifty million you telling me that you will offer me 1million because you are unfortunate right?

Negotiator: please I don't want you to be upset, I beg you.

Bandit: you don't know who I am and what I am capable of doing that is why you are toying with me; I know everything about the people I kidnapped. I have a background knowledge of all of them. I have known this for quite some time now, if not I wouldn't have come to kidnap them.

Do you know where I came from?

Negotiator: no

Bandit: if you think you can get us just track the number and come for us then I assure you I will deal with you and your people.

Negotiator: no, it has not gotten to that.

Bandit: I heard of the attacks you carried out in the neighbouring village regarding the kidnap issue. This will make me unleash my anger on your people whom are here.

Negotiator: listen to me please, let me make a correction here. Nobody was hurt here, nobody launched attack on anyone.

Bandit: what are you trying to say? That I don't know what am saying? I have suddenly become mad.

Negotiator: honestly speaking I am serious, let's just focus on the ransom issue.

Bandit: then what are you saying now? Say something better that will go down well with my spirit. If not allow me to continue with my work.

Negotiator: I have called few people to let them know that you have rejected the 1 million Naira, I was planning to pay.

Bandit: now listen and listen very good; if you ever mention that amount again, I will kill one amongst your people. Fr. Will be the one to confirm it before I proceed to kill him. Because you are taking me for granted, he spoke to you yesterday through me and told you about their ordeal but you are still proving adamant right? You couldn't even call back to check up on them.

Negotiator: no! I called you the network wasn't friendly.

Bandit: listen well it has shown that you don't care about your people whom we have kept captive, I will certainly stop feeding them and whatever care we have been giving them we will stop.

Negotiator: no no no no, it hasn't gotten to that please.

Bandit: how do you mean? I have tried my best; do I know them? No!

Do I have anything in common with them? No!

It is you who know their worth not me therefore do something.

Negotiator: please listen to me.

Bandit: will you keep quiet? You fool, you are nothing but an idiot.

Negotiator: please you will hear from me tomorrow morning. I need you to help me so that I can speak with him.

Bandit: I won't let him speak to you because you are a fool, why will you offer me a million Naira? If you have provided the amount, I ordered you to do then I will proceed to allow you speak with Fr. For now, get out of my phone.

Sixth recording (0: 52 seconds)

Negotiator: you keep ending the call, you hang up without letting me talk. Honestly it makes me feel sad.

Bandit: since you don't have anything meaningful to say to expect me to listen to your conversation?

Negotiator: please I need your help, I need to speak with Fr.

Bandit: you will not hear anything from him you cannot speak with him I thought I told you that.

Negotiator: I need to ask him something important.

Bandit: I won't connect you with him!

Negotiator: please help I want us to come to the end of this negotiation. There are some things that are in his custody, so we need to know where he kept them.

Seventh audio recording (1:57 minutes)

Negotiator: servant of God

Bandit: I can hear you

Negotiator: please help, I beg you in the name of God.

Bandit: I can't see seriousness in you that is why, if you are serious, I will help you.

Negotiator: I need you to understand that we don't have such an amount of money.

Bandit: then I can't help you. If you want me to help you, then help yourself first. What is 5 million? How do you want me to help you by you offering me 5 million.

Negotiator: but the ball is in your court.

Bandit: if you want me to help you then do what is right, I have a lot of things ahead of me.

Negotiator: I did not even solicit the advice and opinions of their relatives and I increased the amount to 5 million they are even worried because they don't know how to raise the money.

Bandit: that is your business, if you like do not raise the money, that's your headache not mine.

Eighth conversation (7:20 minutes)

Negotiator: whatever I'll be saying now is just a plea.

Bandit: what kind of appeal do you want from me?

Negotiator: I just want you to understand me so that we can come to consensus, I need you to understand two things. These people you've held captives are not as wealthy as you think. Secondly, I need you to reconsider, concerning the ransom so that everything will be successful. Because I am equally worried.

Bandit: you are not worried; you are just saying it.

Negotiator: I mean it, I am worried.

Bandit: if you were to be worried, you would have paid the money and brought them out of that dungeon because you all have the means.

Negotiator: to be sincere I mean what I say.

Bandit: what sincerity? Do you even know what it means to be sincere?

Negotiator: I want us to have a mutual agreement between us.

Bandit: hey! Listen to me. I don't have time for your stories or the rubbish you want to spill out. How far with the amount I asked for?

Negotiator: to be frank with you, we don't have such an amount of money.

Bandit: or so you don't have the money, right? Okay just let them be but I promise you; we will certainly execute Fr. Because we have nothing to do with him, he is of no importance to me, you are the one who knows his value and worth not me. If you really need him then *you have no choice than to provide me with what I want.*

Negotiator: when I started this conversation I begged for your cooperation and for you to understand me perfectly well.

Bandit: I don't care about what you want to say, just give me the money I asked for; final!

Negotiator: you know I've honoured and respected you.

Bandit: wait! Did you call me to discuss the ransom money with me, or you called me for useless purposes? Because I have a lot ahead of me.

Negotiator: you know yesterday you said I disrespected and offended you, well I don't want that to happen again.

Bandit: that one is for sure, if you say anything that doesn't go down well with my spirit, your people will suffer for it and I mean it. You know you are not feeling their pains.

Negotiator: I want us to reach a conclusion please, those two children are orphans.

Bandit: who are the orphans?

Negotiator: the younger man (Hassan) and Ummie, Fr. has been the one helping out in terms of their needs.

Bandit: am also an orphan, so don't come around that. Don't try to paint words please I know where you are headed. I won't release anyone unless you give me the amount of money I want.

Negotiator: honestly, we don't have such an amount, I want us to understand ourselves.

Bandit: so, what is the way forward?

Negotiator: I want to talk with some people; you see, Fr. and his boy I want you to release them for the amount of 2 million each, then the others we want to pay 1 million 500 thousand Naira each for them.

Bandit: I don't understand.

Negotiator: but it's self-explanatory, like I said earlier on. 2 million for Fr and his boy, then for the children, 1 million in total 5 million.

Bandit: I want you to understand that we are not here to joke, for us to come for them, means we are fully prepared, listen very well I cannot take that amount from you, I will give you time to think but remember your people's lives are at stake.

Ninth conversation (2:23 minutes)

Greetings

Negotiator so what is the update now?

Bandit: are you okay? Are you supposed to be asking me? Or am I supposed to be asking you that?

Negotiator: don't get me wrong, but I thought we've understood ourselves already?

Bandit: then have you raised the amount I asked you to?

Negotiator: there are a lot of things I want to tell you.

Bandit: then go ahead am listening.

Negotiator: firstly, I want to speak with the people you are holding captive, especially Fr., because there are certain things, he needs to tell us; where they are so we can gain access to them. Until this is done, I'll not know the way forward.

Bandit: oh okay, so you have come up with the money I asked you to raise for me?

Negotiator: I have told you already, our wealth status is not up to that but we'll try our best to see what we can do.

Bandit: it's like you think we are here to joke; you are just deceiving yourself.

Negotiator: nothing like that; not even close to that.

Bandit: If you think we abducted Fr. Just for a little amount of money, then you must be joking, if you really love him, stop joking around and be serious.

Negotiator: we really want him and all of them back.

Bandit: then what do you want?

Negotiator: I just need to speak with him then I'll respond to you in full force.

Bandit: okay no problem, you'll hear from him.

Bandit: He's here now let me give him the phone.

Negotiator: okay thank you very much.

Fr Stephen: good morning, Fr Habila.

Negotiator: good morning, Fr. Stephen.

Negotiator: please you all should continue to bear with use, I want to hear everyone speak so that we can be sure and start heading down with the ransom. How is Oliver? Give the phone to him

(Fr. Stephen passes the phone to Fr. Oliver)

Fr Oliver: good morning, Fr.

Negotiator: how are you? You people should not be offended you all will soon be out of there. We are trying out best. Where is Ummie and Hassan?

(Fr. Oliver passes the phone to Ummie)

Ummie: good morning, Fr. Habila

Negotiator: don't worry, you all will soon be out of there, okay? Pass the phone to Hassan.

Ummie: yes Fr. Thank you.

(Ummie passes the phone to Hassan)

Fr. Oliver: Hassan, I need you all to be strong, we will get you out of there.

Hassan: okay Fr. Thank you.

Bandit: you've heard all of them speak, right?

Negotiator: yes, I have, thank you very much for keeping to your promise.

Bandit: just hurry up and get the money for me.

Negotiator: so, when can I get across to you?

Bandit: you can do that when you want.

Negotiator: okay I will call you by 12pm today

Bandit: okay I'll be expecting your call.

Negotiator: thank you.

12th conversation

1:05minutes

Negotiator: my friend, am so sorry for the inconveniences but I will get back to you today.

Bandit: what did you say?

Negotiator: I said I will call get back to you today.

Bandit: so that means you didn't understand what I told you right? I have warned you not to say anything annoying to me again because the money you are talking about is not reasonable.

Negotiator: please am only but pleading.

Bandit: if you try such nonsense again you know where the arrow will land, you know who will suffer for it.

Negotiator: Sorry I will try to do better please.

Bandit: oh, that's better

Negotiator: I will call you today.

Bandit: okay I'll be waiting

Exchange of pleasantries

Negotiator: I tried calling you throughout yesterday but to no avail. I tried calling you both in the afternoon and night but it didn't connect.

Bandit: okay, so what is it?

Negotiator: it is concerning what I told you, the people said I should plead with you. You know like I said the villagers don't even know that I raised that amount to 5 million. Because I want us to finalize on this case so I asked them the way out and they said I had to wait for them till 7pm, so it was this morning that they told me that they will add up 700 to 800 thousand. I said a big no to them, this is not a matter of such an amount of money. They should say something reasonable so we can all rest concerning the case.

Bandit: please say what I want to hear because I am not prepared to hear all these. Just go straight to the point.

Negotiator: that is where am heading to, so they managed to raise up to 1 million Naira.

Bandit: don't ever pick your phone to call me if, you are not yet ready. You are speaking rubbish and trash. Like you said you feel like washing your hands off the case, wash your hands off the case and allow them to continue. You are nothing but a fool. I have told you if you keep messing with me, I will eliminate Fr. Just conclude on what all of you want. If you don't give me the amount i.e., 150 million I asked for, I will kill all your people.

If you have anything to say, say it now, before I end my call.

Negotiator: honestly, they don't have such an amount.

Bandit: then stop calling me, if you don't have the money. If I had known that this is the reason why you called me, I wouldn't have picked your call.

Negotiator: we just need understanding.

Bandit: don't ever tell me about understanding again.

Negotiator: it's just that I want you to know that am equally a struggler. And since you don't agree with the negotiation then I will go back and inform them

Bandit: if you think I picked Fr. and his people because of such an amount of money then you are deceiving yourself. Listen and listen good, I don't want to ever hear your voice again.

Negotiator: if you don't hear my voice how are we going to continue negotiations? Just pipe down please.

Bandit: anybody that is concerned about Fr and his people just feel free and give the person this contact but as for you, don't you ever call me again.

20th conversation

1min 34sec

Exchange of pleasantries

Negotiator: am pleading with you as usual so we can successfully arrive at a conclusion, you know it is not going to be nice if we keep on going back and forth on this conversation

Bandit: you see what I told you earlier on, we can't go back on it.

Negotiator: but the people told me to plead on their behalf so we can pay the ransom and have our people back, just look into the matter there's always something you can do. All the villagers have brought out their last savings and now they are left with nothing.

Bandit: no penny will be reduced from that amount I have told you.

Negotiator: I have as well told them what you said but they are still hoping if you could come down to an amount we will afford.

Bandit: it's better we negotiate; 15 million Naira is nothing; add something to it your people are already sick so it's up to you.

Negotiator: even their family members are equally sick there are a lot of wailing and crying here so please just consider.

21st conversation

2mins 15sec

Negotiator: you know the conversation we had, I was the one that went the extra mile to add up to the money, the villagers were not even happy because it will be difficult to raise such an amount but I urge them to because it is very necessary.

Bandit: okay then am very sure I told you what you are asking for will not be possible, if you are sticking to that amount then that is your worry, not mine, I prefer to keep those people in captivity than to release them for such an amount

Negotiator: I know what you are capable of doing but like I always say we have nothing just help us out.

Bandit: it is not possible! Period!

Negotiator: this matter is really getting out of hand.

Bandit: I advised you to wash your hands off this matter!

Negotiator: what I actually want you to understand is that since we both started this, we should both end it.

Bandit: get their family members or relatives to do the negotiation with us; remove yourself completely from this case.

Negotiator: okay no worries with that, I will inform their people and get back to you.

22nd conversation

3 mins 46sec

Exchange of pleasantries

Negotiator: I tried reaching out to you by 8pm and 9pm but to no avail.

Bandit: so, what's the update?

Negotiator: you know you said you were going to plead on our behalf so I haven't heard from you since then.

Bandit: anyways before I say anything, Fr is here, speak with him.

Fr. Stephen: Mallam Habila, good morning.

Negotiator: morning Padre how are you all faring? I know it's not easy but continue to bear with us, we are almost done with the negotiation.

Fr. Stephen: I just pray he concurs to what you are saying.

Negotiator: he has tried and successfully we are almost getting to the end of all these, help appreciate him.

Bandit: so, what's new?

Negotiator: I told him to appreciate you, you've done well.

Bandit: how do you mean?

Negotiator: we have some level of understanding.

Bandit: we don't have an understanding yet, we are yet to agree I hope you Know that.

Negotiator: but we talked yesterday and we had some mutual agreement that you will talk to your boss.

Bandit: I told you it will never be possible; the boss didn't agree with that amount of money.

Negotiator: but honestly, we have tried our best, we even need some days to complete the money.

Bandit: 15 million is not the deal so deal with it.

23rd conversation

Negotiator: I called as usual but it didn't connect.

Bandit: like I told you that will not be possible, we need 40 million before we let those people go, that is what the boss said.

Negotiator: let's tell ourselves the truth, you abducted those people without the aim of hurting them, if you had wanted to hurt them, you would have done that the day you invaded their house. And you won't equally hurt them this time they are with you.

Bandit: that is if we get what we want.

Negotiator: I will say this without mincing words, if it is the will of God for them to die in your hands, then so shall it be. And they won't be the first to die in the hands of bandits, we are Hausas and we believe in the will of God, they are missionaries and they came to carry out their humanitarian work. We have tried our best and you can testify to that.

Bandit: yes, and I know believe me if I was the one directly involved in this matter, I would have collected that money a long time ago, that's why I told you I will try my best and see how I can help you and that was why I helped you to converse with my boss concerning the 15 million Naira but he didn't buy that.

Negotiator: these people are not my relatives I don't have any blood ties with them, they only came to work and they've done well and I am a living witness to that for this singular reason I decided to help out, yesterday when we talked of increasing the money to 17 million the money is not even on ground but we are sure of raising it, with the help of God.

If you are not willing to release them, let them be in your custody do as you wish with them.

Bandit: well, it is not in my hands to decide.

Negotiator: even the 3 million added to the 17 million I personally went extra mile to add it up just to reach a final conclusion. From there we can begin to sell some farmlands just to raise the money.

Bandit: well 20 million is not the bargain.

Negotiator: okay, I guess it's time for the villagers to go into fervent prayers. Let thy will of God be done!

Bandit: then it is over we should do as we want with them, right?

Negotiator: what else do you want me to say? I have tried my best please consider.

Bandit: I even told my boss to stick to 30 million but he said 40 million is the least he can accept nothing more nothing less.

Negotiator: I don't have much to say again. Since this matter is getting out of hand.

Chapter Ten

The Voice of The Only Woman Among Us

Healing isn't walking away, isn't hiding. There is so much desire to let it go but it's impossible to let it go of something that inhabits your body. You must see it through. You must nurture it, loot at it from all sides and say, "You are within me. But you are not me"
Emmy Mari

Wounds take time to heal, but healing from a very traumatic experience is quite different and takes a long time, while others never recover. In Ummie's case, she doesn't even know how to explain her situation; she told me severally. Sometimes, she acted normal, but at other times, unconsciously, it's as if she is going mad. After a while, she started to understand and said to herself: oh, am I the one that just behaved this way, "have I acted like this before?" She kept asking me whether I thought she would ever be totally healed of the trauma she has experienced. "Or am I just lining my own pockets? Will it be a total healing or a partial healing like the one I'm experiencing? Because each time I remember what happened, my heart jumps," she says.

"I had a dry throat and a knotted stomach every time I realised; we were in the danger zone (the kidnappers' den). The scary look of the kidnappers, the harsh weather conditions, the hostile environment, the dangerous insects and animals, and the unhealthy food and water we were ingesting into our bodies kept giving me goosebumps and chills because I knew they were harmful and deadly to our health. I started to get fed up with everything, and all of a sudden, I started to conceive bad thoughts and imaginations in my head. What if we were hurt? What if we were killed? What if we were separated from the people we were kidnapped with? The 'what ifs' and 'what ifs' kept surfacing in my poor little head".

I saw her struggle most nights. It was really horrible for Ummie. "When I sleep, I'd usually wake up with a shout, then realise that it was just the experience I'd had before replaying in my head and, after waking up, I'd find it hard to go back to sleep."

Months after our release, I called to check on them, and she was crying. and I asked her why she was crying this time around. She said, "I remember very well that fateful day, while the morning was still young when the kidnappers burst into the house and made their way in. They interrupted our sleep by force and dragged the four of us out of our rooms, out of the house and finally out of the village. They made us walk distances we had never walked before. We walked for hours with beatings every time we made an effort to rest or slow down". I remembered with shock when they wanted to kill you because you could not continue, Father; I recalled the loud, scary voice that said: 'Get up and move, or I'll kill you and leave your corpse here."

We had no choice but to encourage and support Fr Stephen to keep going. What would have become of us if they killed you at that point? She continued to remember what made her cry that morning again. She told me, "I remembered crossing a lot of farmlands with large ridges and a certain river with a high-water level."

It is not easy when I close my eyes sometimes, Ummie told me. What comes to my mind sometimes is the "Periods of rains we experienced which were my worst nightmares, coming into the tent and forcing us to face the wall of the tent, it was very frustrating as every time we did it, our backs hurt. The intimidation, humiliation and death threats were degrading," she recalled.

The most humiliating we all saw of Ummie was the arrival of her monthly cycle. "I shook with fear as the blood poured out of me. Yes, my usual monthly flow had opened the door without even knocking. My lower abdomen hurt, and I couldn't do anything. I couldn't even sit up and spent the whole day lying down. It was frustrating to be in a situation where I couldn't care for myself during that time". It was a difficult moment for all of us, having to watch Ummie in such horrible pain, with no painkillers to relieve her, no sanitary towels, no tampons and no clean clothes to contain her blood. We all watched her cry and moan helplessly. She used dirty rags to support the heavy menstrual flow, she divided the rag into four parts, aiming to use each piece for one day. When the jailers asked us to relieve ourselves, she would take the opportunity to soak her menstrual rag in dirty water. And reuse, of course. The most humiliating thing for her was to find herself with 8 corpulent men in the same tent for the whole of this period, "At one point, I began to have the impression that rotten blood was stinking up the hut, and it turned out to be my menstrual blood."

"The month-long experience was terrible, horrible and terrifying, but our greatest joy was to see that the four people kidnapped that day came back unharmed". She said, "This experience has taught me several things about life."

- God's endless love, mercy and compassion,
- The value of individual and collective prayers.
- The strength that comes from the love, concern, support, affection and care we have shown each other during our captivity,
- The positive energy that comes from optimism, faith and hope.

In her words when I asked her to summarise her thoughts on the state of the country after her own ordeal: “It is indeed sad that the threat of this evil act continues to grow every day, and the sad news is that it is the innocent who are caught in the nest and innocent lives are ruined, but is that really appreciable? It reminds me of the saying, ‘If wishes were horses, beggars would ride’ As far as I'm concerned, I won't just ride; I'll fly. I want the chance to re-sharpen and restructure this homeland of mine. Before reaching such heights, I pray for a better country where its citizens move freely without fear of being hurt, where citizens learn to accept each other as they are and put aside their religious and ethnic differences. Only when these principles are put into practice will the family, the neighbourhood, the school, the workplace, the place of worship, our country, our nations and, indeed, the world as a whole be a better place.”

Chapter Eleven

The Mysteries of Tragedy

Pain has a purpose; if you find it, you will grow. A veil lifts up to reveal the mythical, the beloved poking us only to pull us close.
Bhakti Poems

Like usual, terrible situations that don't seem to have God's fingerprint on them, this rapture doesn't seem to have God's fingerprint on it. This kidnapping experience does not seem to bear the slightest trace of God's hand. That's true on the surface, but it's actually not true on a deeper level. God has shown his great power in many ways. We will discover this in the next stories you are about to read.

Our experience of bandit wearing the rosary

When we arrived, we met four people who were already in their third week. They were captors from ECWA Church Gidan Garba. A Pastor with three of his members; Iliya, Yunusa and Yusuf. The three weeks they stayed was characterised by Tears and Torture. Their breakfast, lunch and dinner were followed by series of beatings. The leader of the bandits in the forest was called *Uban Sulow,* which literally means 'the slow father'. *Uban Sulow* was the most feared and murderous of the bandits, the executioner, the killer and the commander, who ordered the daily beatings of his victims. The first time we arrived, we were beaten. After the beating session, I quietly asked Yunusa how often they were beaten? Once or twice a day he said. I had a deep sigh, and my heart sunk. I could imagine how bruised our bodies were going to be.

After the first beating when we arrived, *Uban Sulow* ceased all our sacred objects; sacred images, medals; rosaries found on our bodies and in our pockets. Some were kept, others thrown away, and *Uban Sulow* wore the finger rosary he ceased from Ummie. On the second day, when we awoke with all the pain of our two-day journey and the beating we had taken, *Uban Sulow* entered the hut where we were chained and asked us to turn our backs. Yunusa, one of the men who had already been there before we arrived, told me that he was about to beat us. My heart sank.

I sat turning my back at him with chains on our legs, expecting to be beaten as usual. All my heart could think about was the beating. The minutes ticked away into hours, and no beating came. I wondered what had happened. The next day, the same thing happened. We were all sitting down, facing the walls, and the beating didn't come. On the third day, the fourth and the fifth nothing happened. Yunusa told me: 'Thank God we were taken away and brought to them. Since we arrived, the beatings have stopped.

On closer inspection, I saw *Uban Sulow, wearing* Ummie's finger rosary, and our other colleagues began to observe very strangely that the same *Uban Sulow* who had been a great terror to them was, in fact, very gentle and kind now. They were all surprised to see how the violent *Uban Sulow* had become so gentle. For us Catholics, this can only be the powerful intercession of the mother of our blessed Lord, whose rosary he was wearing. Our Lady transformed his heart of violence into a heart of peace. From that moment on, he never again sought to harm anyone.

The mysteries of tragedy: Mary Anne's story

This miracle is the most remarkable of all. It sums up the story of Jesus and his super healing powers. Mary Anne, my eldest sister, has not enjoyed good health for the better part of her life because of sickle cell anaemia. As a young adult, she fell ill more frequently and had to have blood transfusions. My sister has had terrible health problems throughout her life. She has faced these illnesses with courage and bravery. Sometimes, I wish I could transfer her illness onto me so that she would feel better.

At the beginning of February 2022, my sister, my mother and her friend, mama Titi, came to my house in Gidan Mai Kambu for the Easter ceremonies. When they arrived at the parish, I ran to the car to welcome them, and I noticed that Aunt Mary-Anne was struggling to get out of the car, helped by my brother Boniface. I immediately felt a mixture of joy and sadness. Happy that they had come to see me for Easter but very sad that my sister could no longer walk.

We struggled to get her into the house, and once again, I saw my sister in pains as a result of the hip problems. In my heart, I said: 'My God, when will this suffering stop for my sister?

Once in the house, we tried to keep a positive spirit to encourage her. She was very dull, and nothing seemed to excite her, which was quite understandable. The next day, I arranged for her to see a doctor at the University Teaching Hospital in Zaria, Kaduna State, forty minutes from my house. She was able to book an appointment with the doctor. After all the diagnosis and analyses carried out by the hospital, the final report from the team of doctors who examined her condition said that both her hips will be surgically removed and replaced. This will cost a total of N10,000,000 ($100,000).

My sister got discouraged, and she became very melancholic. I tried to comfort her, and to make her stand but she couldn't get up. I held her hand and assured her that we would raise the money for her operation. I was making a promise, but I didn't know how I was going to keep it. I made it anyway.

When we got back from the hospital, we continued the Holy Week activities in my parish. My sister made a point of attending all the ceremonies. She moved around in pains while I looked on with strength and courage.

After Easter, my mother, her friend and my sister returned to Katsina to prepare for my younger brother's wedding. Usually, weddings are supposed to be a happy family celebration, but that wasn't the case because my sister was fighting for her life with her hips to be surgically replaced. And it really hurt to see her suffering like that. On Boniface's wedding day, I was the principal celebrant at Mass. Unfortunately, my eyes were riveted on my sister throughout the Mass. I kept seeing how she struggled to stand, to move and to cheer the new couple. I couldn't stop crying throughout the whole ceremony. I kept asking God why my sister had to suffer such pain from the moment she was born.

After the blessing in church, we all went outside for the reception ceremony. Once again, my sister tried to be very present at the reception. We wanted to carry her to where she needed to be. She sat at the reception arena and watched the young couple dance for joy. At one point, I went and sat next to her and encouraged her as usual. I took her hands and said: Auntie, you're going to get better. You've been through the worst of ill health, and you've come through it. This, too, shall pass. These words came out of my mouth, not because I had clear answers about how the money for her operation would be raised. Nor was it because I was convinced that the surgery would succeed. I was simply showing my faith.

That evening, some of the priests and religious who had attended the wedding ceremony invited me for a dinner to congratulate me on the success of the event. It was then that I realised that I had significantly wept publicly for my sisters' poor health. Indeed, while everyone was joyful, I saw myself in a very dark situation, and I wept without being ashamed of people looking. Then I realised that my sister's situation had got the better part of me. The priests and sisters tried to cheer me up, and I also drew strength from their company.

The date for the operation was set, and I asked the priests and religious of the Diocese of Sokoto and my brothers, the MSPs, to pray and offer Masses for the success of my sister's surgery. The doctors informed us that the operation had a 50% chance of success. In the meantime, I asked some of my friends for help, and I was going to sell my cereals to support my sister. It's maize and rice from my farm. The surgery was due to take place on 26 May 2022, and the money from the sale of the grain was brought to me on 24 May at around 7 pm. That was the end of my preparations for the surgery.

During the first week of our arrival, we prayed for everyone and the success of the surgery because it was the last thing I had to do before being kidnapped, and every time we prayed, we raised this intention before God. During the second and third weeks of our captivity, we didn't know what to pray for, whether it was thanksgiving for the success of the surgery or preparation for the surgery.

After 33 days of mourning, on the day I was discharged, she was the first person I saw. I saw her approach me with confidence and gave me a hug. I looked at her straight in the eye, and all I saw was a woman who had been healed, but I didn't yet know how. I quickly asked her: Auntie, how did the surgery go? She immediately replied that God had done it for free. The moment the news of our abduction reached her on her sick bed, my sister rose to her feet and started walking in shock. Now, in a normal situation, the news of my kidnapping should have made her and others collapse. No but the reverse was the case. This for me is one of the greatest mysteries of our unfortunate kidnapping.

The mysteries of tragedy: The story of Mr Okpara

Before Oliver was ordained a deacon, his father, Mr Okpara's illness began, and he underwent treatments and tests to see if he was improving. At one point, Oliver prayed for him to recover a little so that he could be strong enough to attend his priestly ordination. Until his ordination to the priesthood in September 2021, Mr Okpara used catheter to drain urine through his bladder, which meant he couldn't sit in a car or on a motorbike for long, as it could interfere with the processing of the discharge.

Later, Oliver's father complained of swollen testicles and bladder. They went to the hospital for an examination, but there was no improvement; a fortnight later, they returned for an examination. The prostrate became so severe that he had to stop working. When Oliver resumed his pastoral ministry in Gidan Mai Kambu, he went to visit him from time to time, and I have personally gone with Oliver, to see the Dad, together with some members of our Parish. As a parish community, we said Masses for the healing of his father.

At some point, the doctors could not deal with my father's illness. The prescriptions given to him kept burning inside him to the point where he was urinating blood. But we all kept our faith in God, as he did for the woman whose blood began to flow and who was healed.

The prostrate became so difficult for Mr Okpara that at the ABU University Hospital, they suggested that he undergo an operation. My brother, Fr. Oliver Okpara, was terrified for his father, and the father was suffering from high blood pressure. So, they kept an eye on him until they were sure he was ready for the operation. At the time Oliver was worried about the money for the operation. I assured him that I would speak to the bishop about it. All this was going on until when the armed men burst into our presbytery and took us all.

On our return, Oliver was shocked to see his father healed. He said to him, "My son, do you know that the prostrate and the other illnesses disappeared? It was while you all were in the forest God used this suffering to grant me healing" In the words of Fr Oliver: "In fact, God transformed our tragedy into an extraordinary testimony of praise, a miracle that transforms my life, and this testimony becomes the key to my freedom. I am beginning to see his work in my life through this tragedy,"

Chapter Twelve

Tears

"Those tears consoled me in particular and helped me to pick up my pieces"
Sr Cecilia Maundu Focolarina

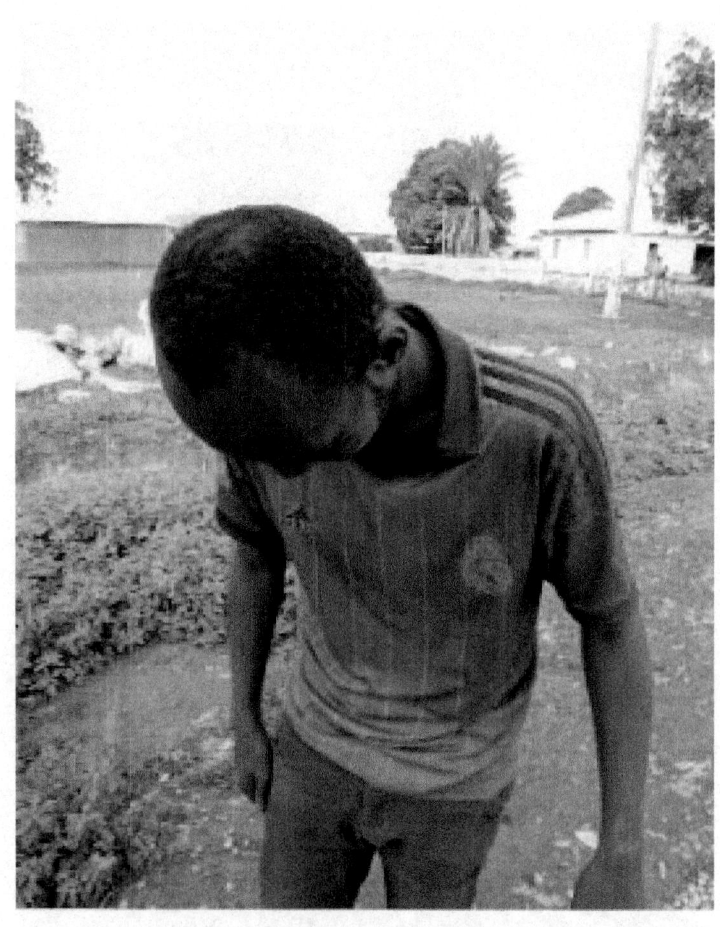

Stephen Ojapah

Fr. Stephen Ojapah, Hassan Fareed Hassan and Fr. Habila Samaila (The negotiator) the day we all regained our freedom.

I was very sad and angry during the days we spent with the kidnappers, and many thoughts of anger and revenge crossed my mind. These thoughts and feelings disappeared when we got out. I began to hear about the hundreds of thousands of people who had stood still in prayer and mourning, waiting for our release. I will never meet many of those friends, from far and near, who shed tears on our behalf. Those tears gave me particular comfort and helped me to pick up the pieces. The wonderful community of Gidan Mai Kambu and the many friends and neighbours around us. The community I met never visited their farms and businesses, going without their daily bread for the 33 days we were away. I heard the story of the children of the parish who prayed against the rain during the days of our absence because, in their minds, every day that it rains, it is likely to fall on us. The children gathered in the church every day to pray for our safe release. These stories had a very positive impact on me when we returned.

Welcome by Bishop Kukah

Oliver Okpara, Ummie Hassan, Bishop Matthew Hassan Kukah, Fr Stephen Ojapah, Hassan Fareed Hassan

Bishop Kukah's role in my life as a priest will be the subject of another book in the future. I cannot dwell on the impact he has had on my life. During the dark days of the Diocese, he supported our parents and all the priests, religious and laity. He was our first point of contact after we left. We arrived in Sokoto to see him. We had understood that a simple ceremony was planned at the chancery to welcome us, but our car had problems on the way and we couldn't get there in time. Finally, we met him at his home at around 7 pm.

When we arrived at his house, he stood in front of the door and didn't hug or touch us. He pointed his hands towards the chapel. When we entered the chapel, we saw the Blessed Sacrament exposed in the tabernacle. He asked us to kneel and spend a quiet moment with the Lord. At that moment, all we could hear in the chapel were sobs and tears flowing freely. After about ten minutes of silence, Bishop Kukah stood up to address us. Bishop Kukah rose to address us. As usual, he began by telling us the story of why the Tabernacle was left open. He said: 'As soon as I heard of your abduction, I went straight to the chapel and exposed the Blessed Sacrament, and I told the Lord that this tabernacle would not be closed until all your children had returned. Now that you have returned, you must come and greet him first. Bishop Kukah then opened his arms and gave us all a warm hug. This gesture meant a lot to me at the time. It rekindled a positive energy in me and many of us, a positive energy that contributed significantly to my healing and recovery.

Our Parents

While we were with the kidnappers, we were worried that when we got out, we wouldn't hear that our parents, friends or siblings had died in shock as a result of the incident, so we prayed fervently. We had the opportunity to pray every day. We prayed for the Diocese of Sokoto, our bishop, the priests, the religious and all the faithful of the Diocese of Sokoto, and we also prayed for the MSP family throughout the world.

. One day, Ummie asked me: 'Am I sure we'll get out of this place alive? I told her that one thing I am sure of is that our names will be mentioned in every MSP-run parish in the world. So, we prayed for them, too. Our dear parents were another great source of worry. We could imagine the crises and suffering they were all going through. For example, Mrs Grace Hassan, Ummie and Hassan's mother blacked out when she heard the shocking news. She couldn't speak, eat or do anything. She couldn't even cry; the pain was so unbearable. Father Oliver's parents are naturally calm people. This period was too traumatic for them. They were elderly people who found themselves alone. Father Oliver was ordained a priest only eight months ago. His parents have been comforted by the visits of many parishioners from St Teresa's Catholic Church in Funtua. My own family, especially my mother, has experienced pain, heartbreak and the death of children. At this stage, she is looking after a sick daughter who needs five to ten million Naira for an operation and a son who is in the hands of kidnappers. My mother's tears were never-ending, but she was brave and optimistic, believing that everything would end in praise. And that's precisely what happened. My mother was the first woman I saw when we were released. When I looked into her eyes, I saw tears, pain, hope and courage.

Friends outside and inside Nigeria

I was lucky enough to have a good network of friends and family outside Nigeria. They all raised prayer banners for us. All the convents inside and outside Nigeria, many parishes inside and outside Nigeria prayed for our safe return. When I travelled to visit my good family friends in the USA, Dan and Tina Dirksen's family who also prayed for our return, they allowed me to see some of their friends and family. Almost everywhere I went, the wishes kept coming. We can't thank people enough. The sacrifices of thousands of people. All over the world. My MSP family and all the parishes they look after have written our names on their daily Mass intentions. This chapter is about the many convents in Nigeria. The many parishes, the friends who knew our parents, many people I can't even remember. Many cried when we were captured and when we were freed, and the photos went viral. They all shed tears for us. Those tears are very therapeutic for all of us, thank you.

Thanksgiving Mass at Gidan Mai Kambu: Bishop Kukah at his best

The community of Gidan Mai Kambu and the entire Diocese of Sokoto certainly held their breath, waiting for us to arrive safely. Two years before our incident, the Diocese witnessed the death of Michael Nnamdi, killed by bandits at the seminary in 2020. Bandits invaded the Good Shepherd seminary in January, kidnapped four seminarians, released three and killed one. The seminarian killed belong to the Diocese of Sokoto. In 2021, bandits invaded St Vincent Ferrer Malumfashi and abducted Father Joseph Keke, aged 75, and Father Alphonsus Bello Yashim, aged 33. Father Yashim was killed within minutes, and Father Keke stayed with them for the next three weeks. All four of us made it out alive, which led to a celebration in the Diocese.

The bishop celebrated a Mass of thanksgiving at Gidan Mai Kambu amidst tears and joy. At the end of the Mass, he did something spectacular. He called all those who had been kidnapped in front of the whole congregation. He took us by the hand and asked us to repeat after him the words he had spoken: *"God our Father, we thank you for the gift of your son Jesus Christ, who suffered and died for us. You are always with us in joy or sorrow. You were there when the kidnappers arrived, you were there with them in the bush, you were there when they were chained, hungry, and even when they were beaten. We offer to Jesus on the Cross all the pain, suffering and humiliation they have endured, and from our hearts, we forgive you and offer all the pain and suffering to you Jesus, praying for their conversion. Amen."* With this singular gesture, Bishop Kukah set in motion a healing process that cannot be explained. Throughout his ministry as a bishop and father, he has always preached non-violence, even in the face of the most brutal provocations. Here is an extract from the sermon he gave at the funeral Mass for Michael Nnamdi, a seminarian from Sokoto who died at the hands of kidnappers in January 2020 at the Good Shephard seminary Kaduna.

"My dear brothers and sisters, Anger and the quest for Vengeance are a legitimate inheritance of the condition of un-redeemed human beings. Both have appeal. Through Violence, you can murder the murderer, but you cannot murder Murder. Through violence, you can kill the Liar, but you cannot kill Lies or install truth. Through Violence, you can murder the Terrorist, but you cannot end Terrorism. Through Violence, you can murder the Violent, but you cannot end Violence. Through Violence, you can murder the Hater, but you cannot end Hatred. Unredeemed man sees vengeance as power, strength and the best means to teach the offender a lesson. These are the ways of the flesh. Christianity part ways with other Religions when it comes to what to do with the enemy. Here, we must admit, Christianity stands alone. This is the challenge for us as Christians".

"Others believe in an eye for an eye, a tooth for a tooth, or that one can take either blood money or make some form of reparation one way or the other. However, for us Christians, Jesus stands right in the middle with a message that is the opposite of all that is sensible to us as human beings. Put back your sword (Mt. 26: 52). Turn the other cheek (Mt. 5:38). Pray for your enemy (Mt. 5: 44). Give the thief your cloak (Lk. 6:29). None of these makes sense to the human mind without faith. This is why Jesus said the only solution is for us to be born again (Jn. 3:3). The challenge before us is to behold the face of Jesus and ask the question, are we Born against hatred, anger, violence and vengeance? There is hope, my dear friends. Are we angry? Yes, we are. Are we sad? Of course, we are. Are we tempted to vengeance? Indeed, we are. Do we feel betrayed? You bet. Do we know what to do? Definitely. Do we know when to do it? Why not? Do we know how? Absolutely. Are we in a war? Yes. But what would Christ have us do? The only way He has pointed out to us is the non-violent way. It is the road less travelled, but it is the only way".

Chapter Thirteen

Trauma and Building Resilience

Like a phoenix rising from the ashes, resilience empowered me to transformed my pain into purpose and my wounds into wisdom

(Sr Cecilia Maundu Focolarina)

Trauma and Building Resilience

Building resilience:

Our journey into the forest for two days and back, with all the pain, beatings, insults and difficulties we encountered, is a journey of resilience. I never thought I'd be able to go back to normal in this life after the tragic incident that occurred to us. In March 2024, I was gathering data on the victims abducted and released in Katsina. I discovered that some of the abducted and released victims could no longer bear the trauma and had died. Nigeria, as a country, is a huge scene of trauma. This cycle of violence and trauma continues. We see it in the clashes between farmers and herders, the extortion on our roads, and the attacks on people in bus stations, markets and public places.

Many Nigerians are injured, and many victims of kidnapping and other forms of violence are licking their wounds with salt and pepper. Family, friends, government and work colleagues continue to experience injury and suffering, even after the tragedy of kidnappings and other forms of violence. The cycle of trauma is real for many. And the support system is not very well developed, in fact in most cases, it is very absent. for example:

The Trauma of Malam Kaisar

Ten years ago, a man from Katsina State in northern Nigeria whom I have kept his identity away and refer to him as Kaisar, for his security was accused of blasphemy. The crowd gathered to kill him on the spot, but the Emir (King of the land) got wind of the story and ordered his arrest in other to be given a 'fair trial'. In the evening the man was due to honour the Emir's invitation. He knew he would not return alive. So, he called his wife and children. He told them that he had been accused of a crime he had not committed but that he felt he would not return alive. He hugged his wife and children, said goodbye and left. Fortunately, six months later, the man was released and reunited with his family. Since his return, he has never been the same. He has become a recluse, never interacting with anyone outside his immediate family. Sometimes, he even isolates himself from his family. Whenever he hears a visitor in the house, he hides until the visitor, whoever he is, leaves. This man's trauma runs deep. There are many Malam Kaisars in Nigeria and elsewhere.

Fear of water

Since I've been freed, I've been able to face up to all my fears, except the fear of water. I've been back to Mai Kambu several times, and I've slept on the bed where I was kidnapped. I stayed in the parish house, prayed in the chapel and walked freely around the house and the community. To help me overcome my fears. I haven't been able to overcome the phobia of water, that has left me traumatised every time I see a big river. One man was kidnapped during a downpour. For him, rain should never fall again in this world. Every time it rains, he feels he is in danger, and his mind races, imagining that they will come back in the rain.

To be resilient in life is to see every tragedy as a unique opportunity to grow and discover more deeply the meaning and purpose of life. Resilience is an attempt to overcome our worst fears and bring out the best version of ourselves, even when all the odds are against us. Resilience is also about turning to friends and neighbours who encourage us with a pat on the back. A gentle, reassuring voice that has to come from friends.

When I fell and couldn't walk Hassan, Ummie, and Oliver cheered me up. They encouraged me to keep going. They shouted my name until their last breath: "Father, get up, please, let's go..." Those words meant a lot. That voice carried energy. Building resilience means building a support system that can pull you through.

Since we've been out, so many organisations have come forward to support and encourage us. Gaudium Et Spes Abuja: A retreat and therapy centre run by Father Mary John Atep of the Archdiocese of Abuja. Peaceful Heart Network Sweden, run by Guinilla, and Inter-Faith Mediation Centre Kaduna, run by Imam Ashafa and Pastor James Wuye, which have become symbols of love and forgiveness for many traumatised people in Nigeria. I cried as I listened to their stories of hard struggle and reconciliation. An ability worth emulating.

Discovering a new purpose in life

Every tragedy in life gives us a unique opportunity to connect with the plight of the community. In March and April 2022, I mobilised my parishioners to visit two communities in Kebbi and Katsina States. These communities had been driven out by Fulani bandits and had taken refuge in neighbouring communities. More than 5,000 people received the food, clothing and medical aid we brought to them. They were abandoned, without food, water or sanitation, and even the hope of a better future. In Zuru, in the State of Kebbi, while we were distributing food, a five-year-old girl died of measles (and the people continued to share the food without worrying about the little girl, who had just died. People have known greater suffering, and the death of this little girl was perhaps just one of their daily sufferings. The trip to Zuru and Jibia, in Katsina State, was more than gratifying. I felt an enormous sense of connection and empathy as we shared what little food and clothing we had, with the victims of the bandit attacks.

We received food, clothing and donations from friends inside and outside the country to show our solidarity with these people. I was delighted to have found a purpose and a meaning in my life. I had planned to visit other regions in the States of Kaduna, Zamfara, Niger and Plateau.

Then, in May, I was kidnapped myself. This incident made me realise the need to provide support for victims of trauma around the world, to help in some way the hundreds of thousands of victims who have been kidnapped and released, their families who have to live with the tragedy and trauma of banditry and other forms of violence.

Providing this support through the activities of the O-Trauma Victims initiative (www.otvi.org) is my greatest joy. It has given me a purpose in life. I love being involved in community initiatives that support other victims of natural and human violence. In March, I spoke to young students from St John's High School here in the UK who were sleeping rough to raise money to help the homeless in Gravesend, Kent.

The young pupils wanted to understand what it means to be homeless. According to Shelter England's December 2023 statistics, over 309,000 people were homeless in the depths of winter. I used my sad experience of being homeless for 33 days to encourage the young boys to get involved in the community. Giving back to the community is undoubtedly a virtue I discovered during my abduction.

Chapter Fourteen

The Evolution of Insecurity (2015-2024)

Beyond Boko Haram

Although the militant Islamist terrorist group, Boko Haram dominated the headlines at the beginning of this decade, the security situation in Nigeria has become more complex than ever. Boko Haram operations continue, albeit with limited capability and reach. Nevertheless, a new form of security threat has emerged.

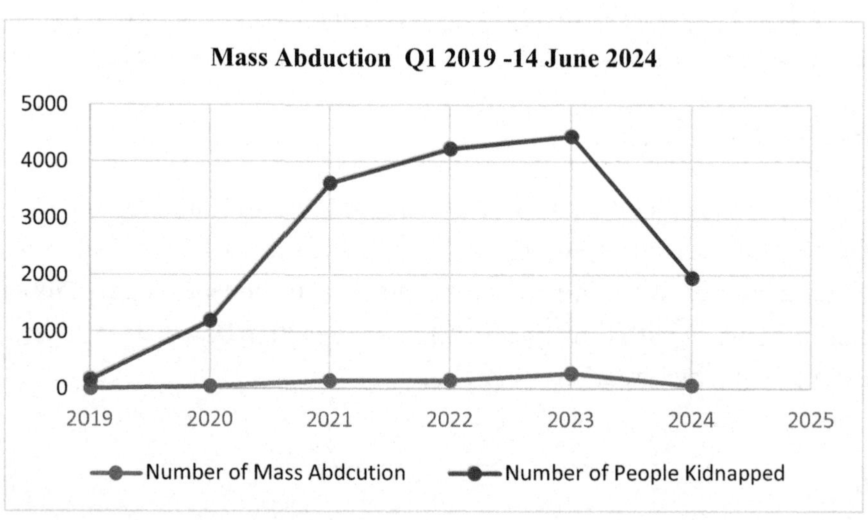

Fig. 5. Mass abduction cases: Q1 2019 – June 14, 2024

Criminal bands have spread all over the country, specializing in kidnappings for ransom. These groups target not only the wealthy and elite but also common people across towns and villages, creating a climate of fear and unpredictability. These kidnappings do not just have an immediate psychological impact on victims (Eloh, 2019), they also disrupt the very foundation of livelihood, leading to families selling off property and assets in order to pay ransom, further straining household financial situations.

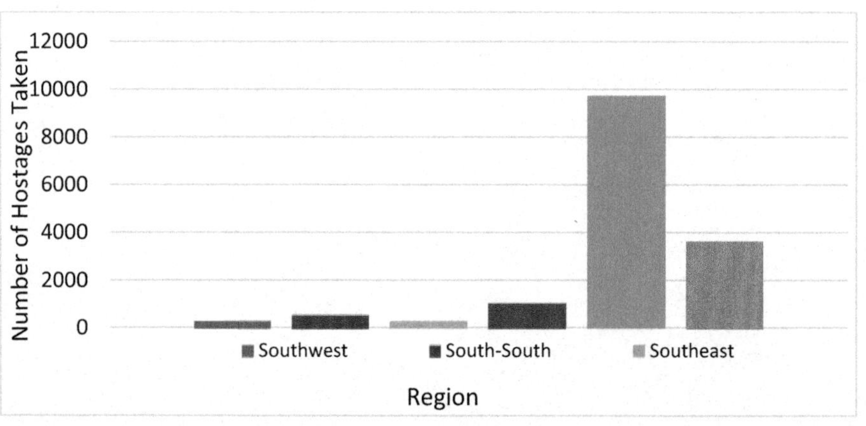

Fig.6. Kidnapping Incident/ Geopolitical Zone: Q1 2019 – June 14, 2024

Nigeria is confronted with a plethora of violent crimes, including banditry, kidnapping, violent attacks, armed robberies and terrorism. The northwest and the north-central have reported the highest crime rates in recent years, but the threat is widespread. Efforts of the men in uniform, some of whom have paid the supreme price, at curtailing these security challenges continue to yield noteworthy results as shown in the graph. Such efforts are noteworthy and must be commended. Of note is the northeast where the Nigerian military has been able to stem the tide of terrorism forcing thousands of terrorists continue to surrender.

In addition, competition for scarce resources, particularly agricultural land and water, has fuelled armed conflicts between herders and farmers. These clashes are rooted in deep-rooted tensions and are exacerbated by climate change and population growth. Banditry, fuelled by easy access to weapons and a lack of economic opportunities, has also become a major concern, particularly in the northwest and north-central regions. These resource-related conflicts and banditry are destabilising entire regions, displacing communities and hampering agricultural production, a sector vital to the Nigerian economy.

Outbreaks of inter-communal violence are often due to historical quarrels or even struggles over limited resources. These conflicts are complex because they can have underlying religious, ethnic and political dimensions. With the significant increase in the availability of weapons and the collapse of traditional means of conflict resolution, inter-communal feuds and clashes have taken a more destructive turn. The frequency and intensity of inter-community violence is a major threat to national unity and social cohesion.

Impact of Evolving Insecurity

Nigeria's evolving insecurity is having a serious impact on the country's progress. The prevailing state of fear and violence discourages foreign and local investors (Jelilov, Ozden & Briggs, 2018). Companies are reluctant to invest in areas considered risky, which hampers economic growth and job creation Ayoola, A. O. (2021). The lack of investment, therefore, creates a vicious circle as the absence of economic opportunities continues to fuel instability and violence.

Persistent insecurity has also led to the displacement of large populations (Ladan & Liman 2021). People fleeing violence abandon their homes and livelihoods, often seeking refuge in overcrowded camps or with relatives in safer areas. In reality, these displacements exacerbate an already resource-strapped scenario and cause social disaffection in host communities. Insecurity-induced population movements disrupt agricultural production, which has a negative impact on the rest of the economy (Ubochioma, Chikaire & Ogueri, Emma, 2019).

Perhaps most worrying is the erosion of trust in government institutions. Most Nigerians believe that the government is not doing enough to address the growing security challenges facing the nation. This perception undermines the legitimacy of the state and hampers its ability to maintain law and order and promote economic development. Confidence can be restored on a number of fronts, including improving security, addressing the root causes of conflict and promoting greater transparency and accountability in government.

VI. The socio-political impact of insecurity

Insecurity, whether due to violence, conflict or crime, strongly affects different aspects of society, including disrupting education, healthcare and social cohesion.

Education

School closures due to violence: School closures due to insecurity are frequent, inevitably making it difficult for children to learn. (Ogona, Kelvin & Goodness, Munachim, 2021). For example, fear of violence, a targeted attack on schools or even the reallocation of school buildings for military purposes can disrupt the learning programme and create a sense of instability. The result is gaps in learning, increased drop-out rates and, overall, a decline in literacy and numeracy skills.

Fear hinders access to education, especially for girls: Insecurity can create a climate of fear, especially for girls and young women. The risk of violence on the way to school or during school hours can deter families from sending their daughters to school. Cultural practices and norms can also restrict girls' mobility, exacerbating the limitations imposed by insecurity. This unequal access to education widens the gap between men and women in terms of educational attainment, opportunities and career prospects.

The Ripple Effect: Disruptions to education have a domino effect not only on all levels of society but also on its political and economic structures. Educated people are the foundation of a healthy economy and community, while less educated people risk remaining poor and vulnerable and perpetuating the cycle of poverty. In addition, a lack of education can make individuals more susceptible to radicalisation and recruitment by extremist groups.

Healthcare

Attacks on healthcare facilities and staff: Insecurity often has direct consequences, such as rapid attacks on healthcare facilities and staff. This creates a dangerous environment for healthcare professionals and deters them from working in conflict zones. The destruction or non-functioning of hospitals and clinics means that communities in the affected area will be exposed to an increase in preventable illness and death (Iqbal, Zaryab 2006).

Limited access to healthcare in conflict zones: Insecurity often disrupts transport networks and infrastructure, making it difficult for people living in conflict zones to access healthcare facilities. This is particularly problematic for people with chronic illnesses, pregnant women and children who need regular medical care. Fear of violence can also prevent people from seeking treatment, leading to untreated health problems and a worsening of the situation.

Devastating consequences: Limited access to healthcare in times of insecurity can have disastrous consequences. Outbreaks of infection can become epidemic. In addition, injuries sustained during the conflict may not be adequately treated, leading to long-term health problems and even death. This contributes to the disintegration of the social systems of communities already facing conflict.

Social cohesion

Increased tensions and suspicion between communities: Insecurity can sow the seeds of mistrust and suspicion within communities. Violence and fear can lead to the disintegration of social networks and, consequently, increased tensions between communities (Chan, Janet 2008). People can become increasingly suspicious of others, whether because of their ethnicity, tribe, religion or other factors. Such ruptures prevent people from meeting and working together for a stable and growing nation.

International involvement

Regional collaboration: The campaign against Boko Haram must not be limited to Nigeria. This understanding was seen as a key strategy leading to regional cooperation. The Mixed Multinational Force (MNJTF) has been set up and deployed in Nigeria, Chad, Niger, Cameroon and Benin to carry out counter-insurgency operations in border areas. This partnership makes it possible to coordinate military operations, exchange intelligence and adopt a unified regional approach.

Humanitarian and development aid: The conflict is directly linked to a profound humanitarian disaster, which has had a direct and indirect impact on the lives of many people. International and non-governmental organisations have played an essential role in providing emergency aid, food security and healthcare to displaced people. In addition, development aid is aimed at rebuilding infrastructure, promoting economic development and strengthening civil society in the regions affected by the conflict. These efforts are aimed at tackling the root causes of the conflict and creating a stable environment.

The challenges of coordination and long-term commitment:

International cooperation is crucial, but collective efforts between different types of stakeholders can be complex. Many of these projects have to contend with divergent political agendas and a shortage of the necessary resources, which jeopardises their success. In addition, maintaining a long-term commitment from international partners is essential to achieving sustainable results, as expectations of them are high after a certain period of time. Donor fatigue and changing global priorities have made it challenging to ensure a regular and consistent level of aid and support.

The factors behind the current security crisis in Nigeria are very diverse in nature. One of them is the high level of poverty and unemployment. For decades, corruption and mismanagement have continued to retard economic development, resulting in multi-level unemployment and a breeding ground for poverty. The lack of hope of achieving goals leads people to anger and despair, making them more likely to be recruited by criminals or radical groups.

In addition, the breakdown of social order is often a key factor in insecurity. For a long time, ethnic and religious conflicts have remained a subtext of the nation's diverse society. Such a climate is conducive to destabilisation and violent conflict, potentially created by elements prepared to use them for their ends. Secondly, the lack of public confidence in formal institutions such as government and law enforcement can lead to a lack of leadership, leaving communities vulnerable to exploitation.

Finally, the proliferation of armed groups and easy access to weapons further exacerbates the situation. Weak border controls contribute to the circulation of illegal weapons, while ongoing conflicts in neighbouring countries are spreading and destabilising Nigeria's borders. These armed groups engage in a wide range of criminal activities, from kidnapping and robbery to insurgency and terrorism, fuelling a climate of fear and instability.

Emphasis on the interconnection between socio-political issues and insecurity

It should be noted that these factors are not isolated from each other but are interconnected at a deeper level. Poverty paves the way for the growth of extremism, while ethnic tensions can be exploited to fuel violence. The presence of armed groups makes economic development impossible, further exacerbating poverty. Similarly, mistrust of the government undermines its ability to address security challenges, exacerbating the breakdown of social order.

These interconnections require a comprehensive and systematic approach to tackling the complex nature of insecurity in Nigeria. The unrealistic model of trying to solve the problem by acting on a single factor is, therefore, likely to be ineffective. It is necessary to link economic development initiatives with efforts to strengthen social cohesion and confidence in government. The proliferation of weapons must be stopped not only by better border controls but also by eliminating the root causes of all conflict and increased violence.

Possible solutions: A comprehensive approach is needed to break the cycle of insecurity in the country. The solution should be to tackle the root causes and promote dialogue and social cohesion. One of the most important measures to take is to explore the root causes of poverty and inequality. This means promoting education and job creation, particularly in areas where these services are lacking. The elimination of corruption and the development of an equitable distribution of resources are also imperative.

Secondly, adequate reform of the security sector is necessary. Strengthening police and military capabilities while emphasising respect for the principle of human rights must always be the top priority. Improved intelligence gathering and effective cooperation between agencies are also necessary. Building a climate of trust between the security forces and the local population is essential in order to share information and work together more effectively.

Dialogue and social cohesion are essential. Promoting tolerance of social, inter-faith and inter-ethnic differences through community engagement and education will be a powerful agent of social cohesion. Social programmes focused on addressing grievances and empowering marginalised groups can certainly contribute to a more peaceful and inclusive society. On a case-by-case basis, tackling the social, economic and political causes of insecurity would ensure a more peaceful and prosperous future for all. We would like to thank the many organisations that have been working in this direction over the last few decades. The Kukah Centre, the Interfaith Dialogue Forum for Peace (IDFP), the Global Peace Foundation Nigeria and the King Abdulla Bin Abdul Aziz Centre for Intercultural and Inter-religious Dialogue (KAICIID).

My Take Away

Hope for future: In the light of all that Nigeria has been for the thousands of people who have been killed, kidnapped and traumatised, I discovered something that must not be lost: hope. Hope is the last resort that no one should lose. I have hope that Nigeria and Africa will pull through one day and very soon.

Life is a journey through nature. The desert is a special place where man meets the divine. The Israelites met God in a unique way in the desert. The prophet Jeremiah met God in the desert. In the midst of wild beasts, the angels served Jesus after fasting for forty days and forty nights, in the desert. So, for me, the unfortunate incident was a special meeting place. I say this in all modesty. It would have remained a special meeting place, even if I had died. But this experience strengthened my convictions about God's saving power at work in human existence.

1. When all the chips are down in life, all we have is God.

When I looked at myself on the floor, in chains, with all the contacts and people I knew, inside and outside the country, nobody could guarantee my safety the next day. None of the big names in my life had the slightest 'importance' at that moment; I was completely at the mercy and insults of the bandits. The only thing I had was God—his reassuring words in the Scriptures, Psalm 23, 91.

2. God may use tragedy for good.

There were a number of things that turned out positive at the end of the day, two of which were told by Father Oliver about his father's healing and my sister's healing. I had brothers and friends in conflict who hadn't spoken to each other for years. The sad event brought them all together in a profound reconciliation.

3. Awareness

Raise public awareness of the trauma suffered by millions of Nigerians.

Before my unfortunate event, I had never been confronted with the reality of trauma. It was always an academic exercise for me, but now I'm very easily interested. One man spent seven years in prison, and since his release, he has opened a special prison ministry, bringing food and other goods to prisoners. Looking back on his actions, it makes a lot of sense to me today.

4. I learnt to be more patient in life.

As a human being, I am filled with so many weaknesses. Some I have prayed and over prayed to get them out of my way. There is one that came in handy while with the kidnappers, and that is patience. I have been kept in the most humiliating circumstances: spat upon and beaten mercilessly. The only reason why I am alive to tell this story is because I said to myself that whatever happens here, learn to be patient with life. This pain, too, will pass.

5. Leah Sharibu

The front cover of this book carries the image of a wailing girl-child. This is a metaphor for millions of victims of violence around the world. Leah Sharibu has been kidnapped and still is with the kidnappers for over 8 years now. I pay a special tribute to her and extend my tears and torture of friendship to her and her parents. For those who died waiting for the return of Leah someday, may their waiting never be in vain.

APPENDIX

Research Methodology

The research employs secondary data analysis to explore the multifaceted issue of insecurity in Nigeria.

Data Collection: OSINT utilization and HUMINT implementation to enhance the quality of the work. The research highlighted ethical and responsible processing of the acquired secondary data.

- Open-Source Intelligence (OSINT): The process of open-source intelligence gathering included reviewing various information sources available to the public like credible newspapers, articles, websites and even social media posts. This included:

  Government Reports and Data: Publicly available documents, statistics and policy papers by the Nigerian government, regional bodies (ECOWAS), and international organizations (UN, World Bank) me was a source of good information concerning the socio-economic and political conditions.

  News Articles and Media Reports: Reputable media properties operating in Nigeria, whether they be local or international, helped by providing focused information about the security activities the actions of the government as well as public discussion about the issue.

Academic Journals and Research Reports: The lengthy scholarly articles by experts on Nigerian security-related matters gave nuanced analysis and historical background that served as a contextual foundation for the understanding of the issues.

Think Tank Reports and NGO Publications: analysis of social and economic issues by Chasuth Intelligence, an independent research and risk management firm, gave ground for the input of the factors which are the drivers of insecurity.

- Human Intelligence (HUMINT): Apart from the data retrieved by OSINT, the HUMINT approach is employed with scrupulous legal and ethical considerations. This included:

  Expert Interviews: Doing interviews directly with the academics, security analysts and journalists helped to access valuable and specific information.

  Country Liaison Network: A Network of contacts gave extra information on local issues added to the research work.

- **Data Analysis and Triangulation**

The data collected through OSINT and HUMINT underwent a rigorous analysis process. First, the thematic analysis was done to bring out the reoccurring themes and the major factors responsible for instability in Nigeria. This study applied the technique of triangulation of data sources to reduce bias and obtain more reliable facts. Through comparison of the data from multiple sources, the study was able to confirm the accuracy and, therefore reduced possible biases.

- **Ethical Considerations**

The work prioritized responsible data collection throughout the research process. When using HUMINT, the consent of the interviewees was obtained, and anonymity was ensured.

Limitations of Secondary Data Analysis

While secondary data analysis offers a valuable approach to understanding complex issues, it is essential to acknowledge its limitations. The work relied on the quality and accuracy of the information available from external sources. Additionally, there were limitations in accessing certain types of data, particularly sensitive information.

Conclusion

The utilization of a varied approach to secondary data acquisition, HUMINT and OSINT techniques, contributed to the collection of a very detailed picture of insecurity in Nigeria. The data analysis procedure, together with data triangulation, made sure that the findings were credible and reliable. This research provides valuable insights for policymakers, stakeholders, and the public seeking to address the challenges of insecurity in Nigeria.

REFERENCES

1. Ayoola, A. O. (2021). Insecurity and Patterns of Foreign Direct Investment in Nigeria (1999-2014). Open Journal of Political Science, 12(1), 28-45.

2. Chan, Janet. (2008). The new lateral surveillance and a culture of suspicion. Sociology of Crime Law and Deviance. 10. 223-239. 10.1016/S1521-6136(07)00210-2.

3. Gylych, J., Ahmad Jibrin, A., Celik, B., & Isik, A. (2022). Impact of Oil Price Fluctuation on the Economy of Nigeria, the Core Analysis for Energy Producing Countries. IntechOpen. doi: 10.5772/intechopen.94055.

4. Iqbal, Zaryab. (2006). Health and Human Security: The Public Health Impact of Violent Conflict. International Studies Quarterly. 50. 631 - 649. 10.1111/j.1468-2478.2006.00417.x.

5. Jelilov, Gylych & Ozden, Kemal & Briggs, Sotonye. (2018). Impact of Insecurity on Investment in Nigeria. 2. 41-61. 10.31039/jomeino.2018.2.3.3.

6. Kogoui Kamta, Frederic Noel & Azadi, Hossein & Scheffran, Jürgen. (2020). The Root Causes of the Crisis in Northeast Nigeria: Historical, Socioeconomic and Environmental Dimensions. Mediterranean Journal of Social Sciences. 11. 95. 10.36941/mjss-2020-0033.

7. Le, Thai-Ha & Bui, Manh-Tien & Uddin, Gazi. (2022). Economic and social impacts of conflict: A cross-country analysis. Economic Modelling. 115. 105980. 10.1016/j.econmod.2022.105980.

8. Modupe Mary, Eloh. (2019). Perspectives of insecurity and the implications on education, physical and mental health in Nigeria.

9. Ndukwe, James. (2023). A socioeconomic analysis of security crisis in Nigeria's development. 10.13140/RG.2.2.14322.68802.

10. Nigeria Labour Force Statistics Report Q2, 2023. National Bureau Statistics. https://nigerianstat.gov.ng/nada/index.php/catalog/75/download/965.

11. Ng, & Ladan, Suleiman & Liman, Sadisu. (2021). Factors responsible for the creation of internally displaced persons and challenges they are facing in Katsina State, Nigeria. Journal of Conflict Resolution. 2. 11-24.

12. Ogona, Kelvin & Goodness, Munachim. (2021). State of Insecurity: Its Effects on Quality and Standard of Education in Nigeria. International Journal of Scientific Research. 473-485.

13. Oguntoye, Mary & Oguntoye, Adenike. (2021). An appraisal of the impact of the oil sector on the Nigerian economy.

14. Oluyemi, Opeoluwa. (2018). Implications of Using the Military and Para-military Forces for Securitizing Nigerian Insecurities: The Case of Niger Delta Crisis. American International Journal of Social Science. 7. 10.30845/aijss.v7n3p6.

15. Omenma, J. & Onyishi, Ike & Okolie, Alyious-Michael. (2020). A decade of Boko Haram activities: the attacks, responses and challenges ahead. Security Journal. 33. 10.1057/s41284-020-00231-9.

16. Ota, Ejitu & Wambu, Chiemela. (2019). International Journal of Social Sciences and Management Review. Under the gun: the military and the rule of law in post-colonial Nigeria.

17. Owoeye, Dada & Nduba, Onyebuchi & Vincent, Ezeanya. (2022). Nigerian Government Responses to the Menace of Boko Haram and Nigeria's Status in the Global Security Rankings (2009- 2019). 5. 60-72.

18. The Constitution of the Federal Republic of Nigeria 1999, S. 14(2) (b). https://nigerian-constitution.com/chapter-2-section-14-the-government-and-the-people/.

19. Ubochioma, Chikaire & Ogueri, Emma. (2019). Effects of Crop Farmers / Pastoralists Conflicts on Sustainable Livelihood Assets and Strategies of Displaced Farmers in Imo State, Nigeria Research Article.

20. Walker, Robert. (2016). Population Growth and its Implications for Global Security. American Journal of Economics and Sociology. 75. 980-1004. 10.1111/ajes.12161.

21. Worimegbe, Powel & Worimegbe, Temitope & Sanjo, Oladimeji. (2020). Income Inequality, Poverty and Business Activities: The Nigerian Experience. 2384-7468.

Reviews at the Back of the Book

In "Tears and Torture..." Fr. Stephen Ojapah recounts his profound experiences of life and service in one of Nigeria's most challenging regions. Over a decade of dedicated work resolving conflicts between Muslim and Christian communities culminates in a harrowing story of abduction that redefines his perspective on life and faith. With deep personal insight and poignant storytelling, Fr. Ojapah takes readers on a journey through the highs and lows of his mission. From his humble beginnings in Gidan Mai Kambu to engaging in peace-building projects and addressing the socio-economic disparities that plague Nigeria, his narrative offers a unique window into the resilience and hope that characterize his work.

The book delves into the darkest moments of Fr. Ojapah's captivity, where every day was a test of endurance and faith. Yet, through these trials, he emerges not as a victim but as a victor, finding strength in the Scriptures and the unwavering support of his mentor, Bishop Kukah. This compelling memoir is more than just a recounting of past events; it proves the human spirit's ability to overcome adversity. It sheds light on the broader issues of governance and security in Nigeria, providing valuable insights for readers worldwide. It is a story of courage, faith, and the enduring power of hope in the face of unimaginable challenges. Fr. Ojapah's journey will inspire and educate, offering a deeper understanding of a world far removed from our own, yet profoundly connected through the universal experiences of suffering and triumph.

Bishop Gerald Mamman Musa, Katsina Diocese, Nigeria

In the English diocese to which I belong, we have been blessed with a good number of fine Nigerian priests – of which the priests of the Missionary Society of St Paul are excellent examples. Also, in the parish where I served before, I was made a bishop, nearly half the congregation were from Nigeria. I learned a lot from their deep faith, their commitment and the public witness that they gave. Through these means, I became particularly aware of the scourge of terrorism and kidnapping, which has afflicted Nigeria for many years. Even so, this remained a largely abstract idea to me, as the reality is difficult, perhaps impossible, to imagine for anyone who has not experienced it – either personally or on the part of people we know well, such as family and friends.

For me, the greatest value of Fr. Stephen Ojapah's account is that it is not only a first-hand experience but also vivid and detailed. He brings to life the sufferings and deprivations of him and his fellow-captives, as well as the anxieties and dilemmas faced by their families and those who seek to negotiate their release. He also quotes extracts from the accounts of other captives and from some of the telephone negotiations that took place. This goes a long way towards bridging the distance between us, the readers, and those for whom such experiences are a brutal reality. Only in this way is there any prospect of motivating the political action needed to make such things, eventually, a thing of the past.

Also important is Fr Stephen's insight into the bigger picture, in terms of the history of kidnapping in Nigeria, and its wider social impact. As an expert in relations between Christian churches and in inter-religious dialogue, he has an ability to understand the situation and motives of people of differing perspectives. Applying this to the very different context of kidnapping, he is able to give significant insights into the attitudes and motivations of his captors – while of course in no way excusing the crimes he describes. He also reflects on his own experience after release, recognising the trauma that he has suffered and sharing what he has learned from ministering to other victims.

Overall, Tears and Torture brings home the seriousness of the problem and the long-lasting trauma that results, for the survivors and for their families and friends. It also gives hope that, with faith and a vision of what is possible, a way forward may ultimately be achieved.

Bishop Paul Hendricks

Auxiliary, Archdiocese of Southwark

United Kingdom

Father Stephen's book is a tapestry of the Nigerian life today, his own story reflects the circumstance of a nation with so much potentials but plays below its capacity. His witness to history on the Boko Haram and insecurity situation is a seminal insight that should be embraced with a view to providing solution. This material is sure a reference piece.

Useni Rufai

Arise TV Presenter

The Morning Show

Tears and Torture presents the injustices of the political system in Nigeria. This establishment allows the immoral and barbaric members of society to further impoverish those who are struggling to bring equality and democracy to a country rich in resources but poor in leadership. Father Ojapah's traumatic captivity exhibits how we must rely on our faith during all our trials. This story heightens our awareness to the simple gifts God gives us each day and even in the presence of evil, we can see that it is God who sustains us. I suggest you read, reflect, and rejoice in the good that has transpired through the sufferings that have been offered for the glory of God. Continue to pray for Nigeria and its citizens as it battles the atrocities as a result of their self-serving leaders.

Mrs Tina Dirksen

Religious Educator

Catholic Diocese of Lafiyatte

Indiana, USA

Once I started reading the book "Tears and Torture… " By Fr. Stephen Ojapah, I couldn't stop in between. The description of Nigerian life, and the vicious circle their lives are caught in is very pragmatically depicted by Father. The realities of his kidnapping bring tears to my eyes, they were the times I can never forget. Praying together for his release from different parts of the world, we KAICIID fellows came together many times with a hope to be of some support. The system is so paralyzed, it gives a sense of fear. My salute to Father Stephen for keeping courage during the captivity and after release in regaining life to the fullest. I sincerely pray that his words bring peace, prosperity and protection to people of Nigeria.

Kenu Agarwal,

KAICIID International Fellow,

India.

Fr. Stephen Ojapah's work is many things together. The author walks the readers through the discovery of Nigeria's social, cultural, and religious fabric, sharing insights and accurate information on the extremist violence facing the Nigerian population, especially the Christian communities. The courageous account of his kidnapping sheds light on the darkest dimension of this violence, which remains largely unknown or disregarded on the international level. As a leader, he shows the way forward to address the predicament of his country, calling at once for security and inter-religious dialogue to be strengthened. Fr. Stephen offers to all of us a unique witness and many lessons about human existence. His book cannot be missed.

Emiliano Stornelli

Chairman, Religion & Security Council (RSC)

Rome, Italy.

Stephen's book, Tears and Torture, is an incisive reflection of his personal encounter with the dregs of Nigerian society, a people who have taken the laws into their hands to inflict pain and misery on other Nigerians. More broadly, it is a deeper reflection of what Nigeria has come to be in the process of modernisation. It equally demonstrates very clearly the failure of the Nigerian state, and the weakness of other organs to interrogate and debunk a systemic culture of superiority of one group over the other. I recommend this book to students, pastors and policy makers.

Fr. Atta Barkindo

Executive Director

Kukah Centre

"Tears and Torture" chronicles the horrible kidnapping experience of Father Stephen Ojapah, a priest working for inter-religious reconciliation in some of the most difficult areas of Nigeria.

In his writing, you see the hand of God guiding, touching, and encouraging him as he and his 3 colleagues are taken at gun point in the middle of the night and forced into 33 days of capacity. Ojapah recounts giving his shoes to a young woman, so she didn't have to continue the trek through the forest barefoot, his concerns for the wellbeing of his cellmates, risking his own life to protect the group, fighting to stay alive amongst dangerous reptiles and insects and surviving horrendous hygiene conditions.

Father Stephen tells us of his efforts to find the humanity in his kidnappers, hoping for empathy and instead receiving beatings and insults. He learns about the kidnappers' lives in the bush, how young most of them are, their use of drugs and alcohol, how they played a wide range of songs all day long from the phones they had stolen, and the reassurance the group felt when hearing a Gospel song.

As they hung to life, the group remained anchored in the word of God, reciting 'Hail Mary', psalm 23, and John 10:10, conducting the Holy Mass, and praying continuous, individually and collectively, not just for themselves but also for their family and friends back home, that none 'should perish from the shock of hearing of their abductions'

Father recounts his 'daily battle between despair and rage' while in captivity and the comfort of coming home to the knowledge of having been held by a world community. He describes where he found the energy to begin the healing and recovery process, even forgiving his captors. Friends, who shed tears on his behalf, gave him 'particular comfort and helped him to pick up the pieces'. Ojapah also highlights the role of Bishop Kukah, an anchor and mentor in Father's life, keeping the Sacred Tabernacle open while he was captured and the steadfastness of his commitment to non-violence, despite the brutal context that so many Nigerians experience.

Nathalie Al-Zyoud

Mediator

Printed in Great Britain
by Amazon